ANALOG MARKETERS, YOUR CAREER IS OVER

A lot of people are terrified of digitization.

TV executives are wondering whether their stations have a future.

Newspaper barons say their industry is 'in freefall'.

A generation of advertising executives are sensing that their career is in the toilet.

At Wunderman though, we have no such concerns.

We have a very clear appreciation of what digitization is bringing to marketing.

This book sets out our perspectives, observations and our insights.

They are based on web analytics, user observation and hard, current data.

You may of course choose to disagree with them.

And stick with the analog marketing principles you have grown up with.

But those principles come from a world that no longer exists.

And they were created to direct media choices that are no longer possible.

So to stick with them if you will.

But you will be making the same choice that losing generals have been making for centuries.

To march into the next war, intending to fight the last.

The analog world is dying, as highly segmented brands find it more and more difficult to connect with **narrow target audiences** via **blunt mass media** and as consumers spend more and more money on **devices and services that eliminate advertising** from their lives. (page 5)

But marketers are struggling to adopt digital because what it does looks to them **nothing like marketing.**

But that's because the concept of marketing was first coined in 1960 to explain the effects of cheap, mass television.

Marketers didn't select TV as their medium of choice. Marketing was invented to explain the effects of cheap TV. (page 9)

To think digital, marketers need to **completely erase** what is in their heads.

They then need to use the following **principles:**

1. Most analog marketing hits the wrong people, or the right people at the wrong time. Digital is more efficient and more impactful because it can hit **only the right people, and only at the right time.** (page 14)
2. There are many digital media. But the most powerful is **digitally enhanced word of mouth**. Use it with care though – you can't use it to *buy* your way to success. (page 21)
3. In the analog era, marketing was about getting people to *think* things so they might *do* things. Digital media are interactive, so now it's the other way round. **Marketing is now about gettin people to do things.** (page 27)
4. There's no point using really smart searc marketing if you don't spend as much tim thinking about what happens **after the clic** (page 31)
5. No consumer will wait 10 seconds for a bran website to download. **Keeping people waiting i a sin.** (page 36)
6. **Most marketers are dataphobes.** And with goo reason. Digital data streams can paralyz marketing departments unless they are handle expertly. *So handle data with care.* (page 40)
7. Digital media will continue to evolve rapidly fo the next twenty years. So **don't wait for the dus to settle.** Marketers need to adopt a permaner beta mentality in their marketing planning. (pag 45)
8. Why find a new customer when you already hav one. Smartly managed, **digital relationships ca last a lifetime.** (page 54)
9. In the digital era, all brand owners are also medi owners. Save media money and **find the perfe partner.** (page 59)
10. Web 2.0 is all about consumers working togethe Work out how to collaborate with them too in **th channel of we.** (page 66)
11. In the analog era the point of much marketin was to encourage consumers to trial a product c

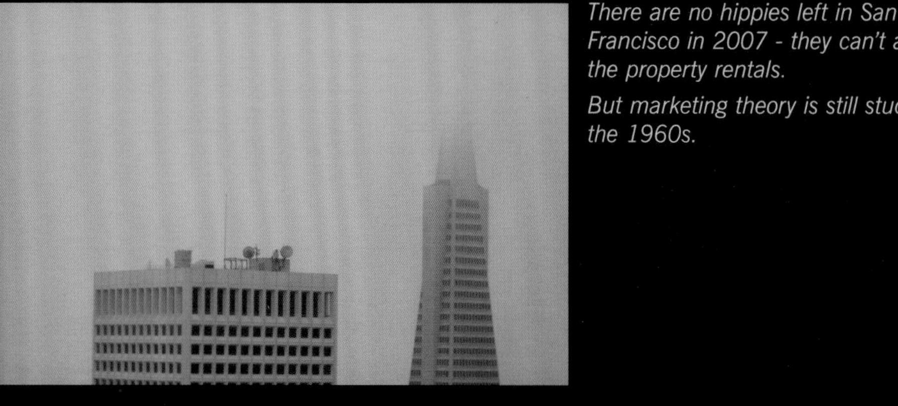

There are no hippies left in San Francisco in 2007 - they can't afford the property rentals.

But marketing theory is still stuck in the 1960s.

service. In the digital era, we can be more direct. Trial can be our startpoint, not our endpoint. **Experience is the best form of marketing.** (page 75)

12. **Handle privacy issues carefully.** You don't need tons of information about a consumer to influence them. Quite often, all you need is *one key piece of information.* (page 80)
13. Digital media are already much more efficient than analog media. But Web 3.0 and Web 4.0 will be much more efficient yet again. **Digital media need to evolve.** (page 87)
14. **Work on predicting the future.** Marketing and media are now moving faster than you think, and much faster than your company can respond to. (page 94)
15. Build a **closer relationship with the truth.** Because in the digital era, the people who tried your service yesterday are talking to those who are trying it tomorrow. (page 100)
16. The consumer has worked out how to use the internet to cut marketing out of their decision making processes faster than marketers have learned how to use it to stay in control. So **the consumer is in control – for now.** (page 104)
17. There is a lot more demand to be had for **products and services that can be delivered instantly** than for things people have to wait for. (page 108)
18. **Boring isn't boring at the moment of truth.** This is vital news for the financial services and life insurance companies that have seen their marketing more than anyone else's ignored by empowered consumers. (page 113)
19. The world is globalizing slower than you think. **Localization is much, much more than just translation.** (page 116)
20. Many things were better when they were analog. **Just because it's digital doesn't mean it's better.** (page 120)
21. *'All warfare.'* said Sun Tzu, *'is based on deception.'* In the analog era, everyone's marketing strategy was obvious. Not so today - **so keep yours secret.** (page 124)

WHY ANALOG MEDIA NO LONGER WORK

Back in the 1960s, in the heyday of television advertising, few brands advertised on television apart from foods and household products.

So demand for airtime was low.

You could launch a brand with a 5,000 rating campaign.

And still have money left in your marketing budget.

Your ads got noticed too.

Consumers had no Xbox, no internet, no cellphone, no text messages, no Gameboy, no MSN and no Google to distract them.

They couldn't even change channel when the ads came on without effort.

Because no one had remotes before 1978.

The result?
Tell consumers a hundred times a year that you could fix their tense, nervous headache, and they all popped your pill.

Sing repeatedly about your golden flakes of corn and that's exactly what they ate for breakfast.

Repeat, repeat, repeat really worked.

No longer

But the economics of TV advertising have changed out of all recognition since the 1960s.

In the US, Japan and Europe, real consumer incomes are now two to three times higher than then. And so consumers have two to three times as much money to spend.

Everyone wants their attention.

Banks, computers, mobile phones, ringtones, insurance companies, vacation destinations and utilities all fight for the same ratings.

And so the amount of TV an individual advertiser can afford has collapsed.

Segmentation hasn't helped either

In the 1960s, most brands were mass market brands.

A deodorant like Right Guard targeted men, women, young and old - over sixty percent of society. It could use TV economically, because over sixty percent of its TV advertising hit its target audience.

But since the 1960s, everyone's favorite marketing strategy has been *segmentation.*

The skin cream that makes a sixty year old woman look fifty.

The bank account for people earning $80K+.

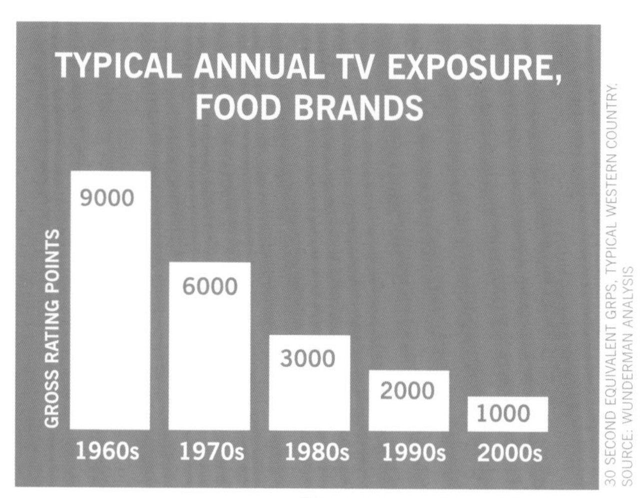

The amount of television big companies can afford has fallen and fallen.

The car for people with three or more children.

Segmentation means smaller, narrower audiences.

Which on a difficult-to-target medium like TV means more and more wastage.

A brand which targets ten percent of society can't use TV nearly as economically as one that targets sixty percent - because as much as eighty to ninety percent of its advertising lands on the wrong people.

And that has made analog media even more expensive.

The wrong ads to the wrong people at the wrong time.

Avoidance technologies have caused more problems

When marketing was first invented, the only way to watch TV was live, ads and all.

Today, many people pay to watch movies ads-free on cable or satellite.

Or they buy and watch DVD box sets.

Or download shows to iTunes.

Or movies to their Xbox 360.

Since 2003, consumers have been spending more on devices and services like these that *avoid* ads than the entire advertising industry has been spending on media to reach them.

And so the model is broken

The rise in demand for TV airtime, combined with the much narrower target audiences brands have today, plus the increasingly effective attempts consumers make to avoid the ads have changed the game.

Brand images don't move the way they did in the sixties.

The transition from press to TV was just as difficult as the transition from TV to digital today.

'Why try to squeeze 120 words into sixty second spots,' asked advertisers in the early 1950s, *'when my full-page newspaper ads can carry 3,000 words of hard-selling copy?'*

Awareness doesn't rise as fast.

Shoppers no longer clear supermarkets of a new product just because it is advertised on TV.

TV has moved from being cheap and awesomely effective, to overpriced and results-free.

It is easy to come to the conclusion that if analog TV was to be invented today, at today's prices, no one would use it.

So switch to digital

Of course the big alternative in marketing today is digital.

Digital has been here since 1995.

And you'd have thought that there would have been a huge switch over to digital marketing amongst big brand marketers.

But most big brands still spend the bulk of their money on television.

Even though many younger consumers spend more time in front of mobile phones, consoles and web browsers.

Why?

The problem is that cheap television was not the only big invention of the 1960s.

The concept of 'marketing' was invented then too. (The word was first coined in 1960.)

Because they were invented at the same time, the effects of cheap television and 'marketing' became one and the same:

Other analog media have problems of their own.

TURN ON, TUNE IN, DROP OUT

'If you can remember the sixties, you weren't really there', say ageing cool people.

Their implication is that they spent the decade fighting for world peace and attaining cosmic nirvana on a cocktail of mind-expanding drugs.

Here's how it really was:

- The best-selling recording artists of the late 1960s were not the Beatles or the Rolling Stones or the Beach Boys. It was the boy band created for the TV series 'The Monkees'. The biggest influence on young people in the 1960s wasn't Bob Dylan, or Malcolm X or Andy Warhol. *It was TV.*
- In 1967, George Harrison of the Beatles heard about the summer of love in San Francisco, and took a plane ride to check it out. He reported back that he found nothing but a few doped-out spotty youths. Even in San Francisco, most young people in the 1960s weren't out in the parks playing guitars with flowers into their hair. *They were inside watching TV.*
- Similarly, audience measurement records from the 1960s reveal that most young French people did not really spend the sixties throwing paving slabs at riot police. *They were at home watching TV.*

The reality is that most young adults spent the 1960s *glued to the tube.*

And that was what made mass media marketing in the 1960s massively effective.

- Marketing became about repeating simple messages over and over. *Because cheap TV let you do that.*
- Marketing was about getting people to *think* things in order to make them *do* things. *Because that was how television worked.*
- Marketing became about building a brand image. *Because that's what happened when you gave your brand 10,000 ratings a year.*
- Marketing ignored the effects of word of mouth – *because consumers lacked the means to spread it beyond their small circle of friends.*

And so today, when marketers set out to 'market', they set out to deliver the effects of cheap television.

Even though we haven't had cheap television for three decades.

Marketers are addicted to television advertising because the concept of marketing was invented to reflect and intellectualize the effects of television advertising.

And so

This book aims to help marketers to rethink what is in their heads.

And wean them off their intellectual addiction to TV-led thinking.

Digital cameras took just five years to kill film.

Digitization will take no longer to kill marketing as we know it.

Back in the nineteenth century, Lord Leverhulme remarked that he thought at least half of his advertising was wasted. His dilemma, he said, was that he didn't know which half.

Today's analog marketing, which uses mass media to communicate to highly segmented audiences is so wasteful, it would make him turn in his grave.

THE 21 PRINCIPLES OF DIGITAL MARKETING

1. TALK TO PEOPLE AT THE MOMENT OF TRUTH

Anyone running for President of the United States spends most of their media money in the last three months before the election:

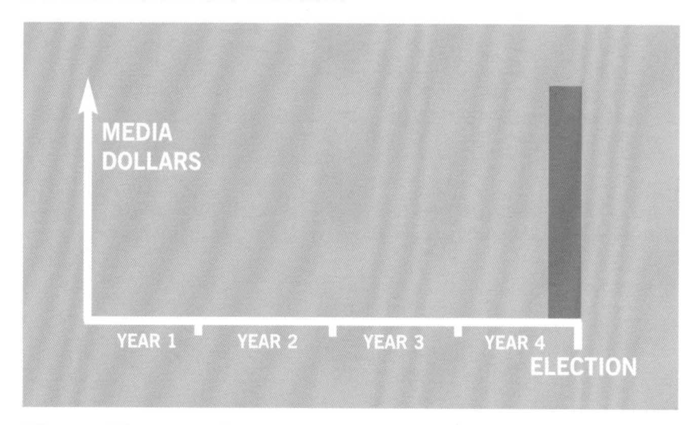

They will argue that any money spent earlier is wasted.

A brand marketer promoting a car will spend their money in a very different way.

Like a U.S. president, a car has typically a four-year purchase cycle in many countries.

But seen from the viewpoint of *the buyer of that car,* a brand marketer will spend their money like this:

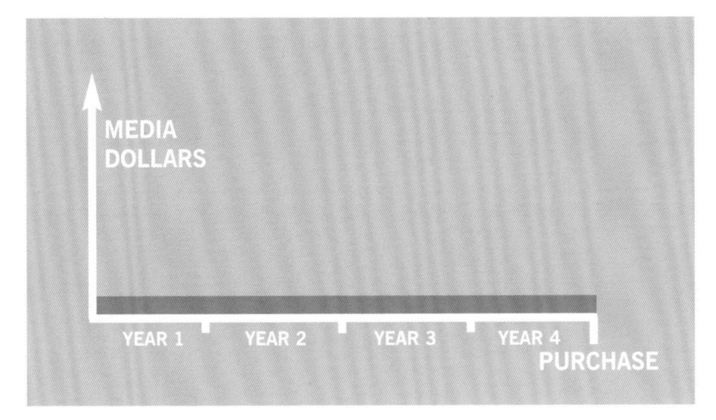

Is this sensible?

Ask the politician and they will argue that money spent in the first eleven quarters is wasted.

Ask the marketer what the first eleven quarters are about and they will say it is about 'long-term brand value development'.

But the funny thing is that whilst all marketers talk about 'long term brand value development', any marketer who can spend their money like the politician does so:

- No home and garden products company spends its money in the fall. It puts it all in the *spring,* just before the main gardening season.
- Similarly, few toy advertisers put their TV money in

Eighty percent of people don't have a dog, so eighty percent of the consumer attention most analog dogfood advertising attracts is wasted.

Billboards should become more effective media once they become programmable by daypart.
For instance, why advertise liquor in the morning?

February. They put it all *just before the holidays,* when parents buy their kids presents.

- No marketer launching a new product advertises it before it's in stock in the shops*. They don't spend before they have full distribution.

The reality is that the car manufacturer believes in long term branding because this is the only way analog TV will let him spend the money.

As digital media become more important though, *this belief is no longer necessary.*

Permission and search marketing pick up people above all in the final three months of their purchase cycle.

They allow a brand marketer to put most of their budget into the final three months before the consumer buys their new car.

If you buy the brutal argument that all money spent before this final three month period is money wasted, then digital targeting creates a *ten-fold increase* in the money spent when it matters, and therefore a ten-fold increase in efficiency.

And it is this promise of marketing *tightly focused on the moment of truth* that will kill analog media.

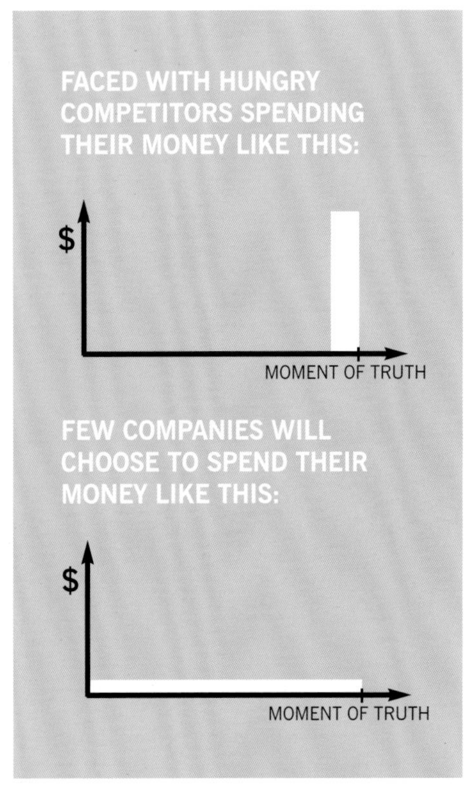

The brutal logic that will kill analog media.

Digitally targeted TV

Digitally targeted TV is still being developed, as digital media companies feverishly work on targeted ad packages to download into DVRs.

But the result is already visible when you look at a

* *Apple's 2007 U.S. launch of the iPhone was an exception: Apple wanted* ***hype.***

page of analog classified ads from a newspaper, and compare it with a page of search results from Google or from Windows Live Search.

Or increasingly from the smart graphical banners delivered by DoubleClick or by 24/7 Real Media.

Whatever you are looking for, the page of analog classifieds is mainly irrelevant, no better than spam.

But *all* the results on a search page are relevant to what you want.

So in the digital era, marketers need to think less about wasteful broad media planning, and more hitting *exactly the right people at exactly the right time:*

A page of analog classified ads gives you very few people who can fix the pipe that's spraying water into your loft.

With search ads, every single result on the page is somehow relevant to your need.

1. Forget demographics

Most marketers define their brand's core media target by demographics.

But this is just a hangover from the TV era.

Digital media use *behavior* to hit people much more efficiently.

If you are selling LCD televisions, your core target is not men, or people aged 25 to 35 or ABC1s.

It is people who are actively researching a planned LCD television purchase.

In the digital era, marketing is getting back to basics.

Your core target is the people who are thinking of buying from you.

2. Offer solutions when they have problems

Washing machine manufacturers advertise in vain on

The graphic of the little man surrounded by media devices has been used to 'explain' digital for ten years now. But it misses the point. Digital is about talking with just the right people at just the right time. The gizmos are incidental.

analog television because no one cares about washing machines.

The only time when people do care about washing machines is when theirs is broken.

Getting their attention is easy when their machine is flooding their apartment.

That's when you should hit them.

3. Forget the long term

Why talk about decade-long brand building any more anyway?

Yahoo became a global brand within two years of its launch; MySpace and YouTube took less.

In today's connected world, brand building is something that happens rapidly, or not at all.

IT DOESN'T TAKE SO LONG TODAY TO BUILD A GLOBAL BRAND

	Period	Years
Coca-Cola	1920-1970	50
Ariel/Tide	1968-1998	30
Yahoo	1995-1998	3
Google	1998-2000	2
YouTube	2005-2006	1

In the online age, it takes a lot less time to build a global brand than in the past.

2. THE MOST POWERFUL MEDIUM IS WORD OF MOUTH

In the analog era, consumers lacked the means to spread their opinions beyond a few friends.

So word of mouth was never that significant.

In the digital era though, word of mouth is very different:

- Product scares spread like wildfire via email, blogs, texts and social networking sites. If you don't handle the issue within six hours may have to explain yourself to *millions* of worried users.
- One bad review on an e-retail site can damage sales of your product. Five bad reviews, and your brand is dead.
- Positive brand news also spreads very fast: third party developers on FaceBook report that their

applications can attract large numbers of users *within hours.*

- Some communities, like the world's six million software developers, are so closely linked that something known by one of them is rapidly known by all.

This means that word of mouth is now an incredibly powerful medium – a medium that can act positively, or negatively for a brand.

Marketers struggle to use digital word of mouth though, because they don't know how it works.

Journalists talk about virtual worlds where people from across the globe will develop closer affinities to each other than to their fellow country people.

Software developers are already there.

Analyzing digital word of mouth

Recently though, Wunderman Network partner VML in Kansas City has developed a tool to analyze digital word of mouth.

It does it by analyzing the links between blogs, websites and other e-media, and by working out what influenced what.

It allows us to study precisely the development of an issue online, and see how it moves forward.

The tool is called SEER™, and SEER™ has some very interesting insights:

- All blogs are not the same: 10% of blogs produce 90% of the influence. Some, like *scobleizer.com* from former Microsoft employee Robert Scoble have produced more influence in recent years than 1,000 similar blogs.
- Similarly, the *Fake Steve* blog that imitated and parodied the announcements of Apple CEO Steve

In the digital era, word of mouth can travel like wildfire.

Jobs has had in some cases an impact comparable with that of Steve Jobs himself.

- Blogs with a salacious content, like those written by people who claim they are upscale call-girls also have a large following. Especially amongst software developers.
- The key measurement is the *connectivity* of an audience. Word of mouth spreads slowly amongst the over fifties because they don't check their email that often. It spreads like wildfire amongst teens because they spend their lives online.
- Nothing travels faster than bad news. However, not all criticism matters. The comments on YouTube about Paul McCartney's 2007 *Dance Tonight* song were mainly negative. But the people writing and reading the comments weren't the people who were going to buy the song.
- Angry people aren't always influential. The most angry postings on Amazon.com rarely get rated as 'useful' by other users. If you want to be influential, *cut the swearing and use whole sentences.*
- When consumers discuss an issue, they rarely discuss brands. It may be your market, but *it's not necessarily about you.*
- Word of mouth is global, but spreads faster between countries that share a language. An online rumor will spread more rapidly from Madrid to Buenos Aires and Miami than it will to Paris.
- Digital word of mouth fills the gaps left by

In England in the early 1900s, Beecham's Pills used word of mouth to let people know they were recommended by the King's doctor.

Today, word of mouth can travel through the planned use of digital media.

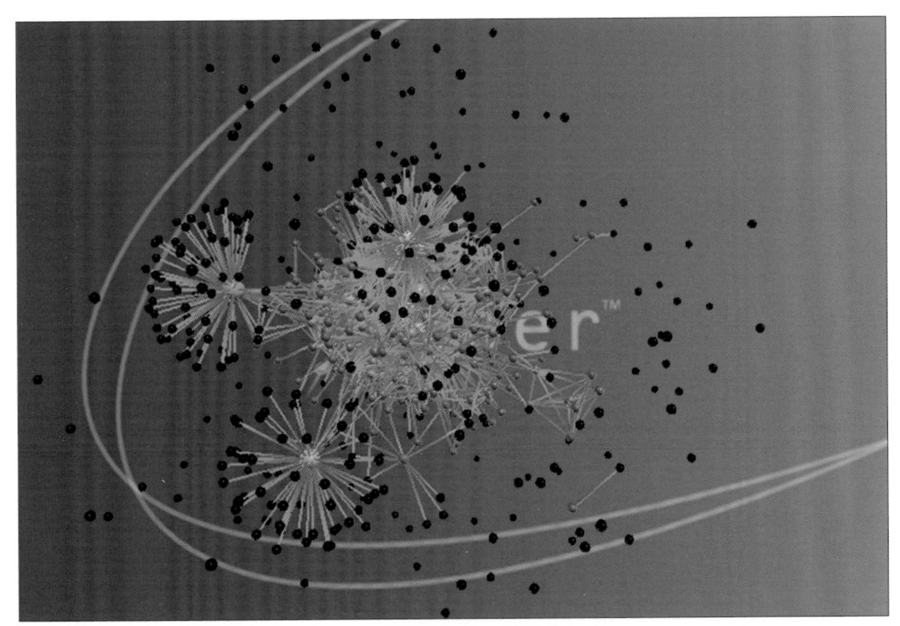

Hyperlinks, and the directions of those hyperlinks, allow SEER™ to track down online ideas and influences to their source. SEER™ analysis reveals that many online issues have some quite surprising startpoints.

Here SEER™ explores how an automotive issue has developed online.

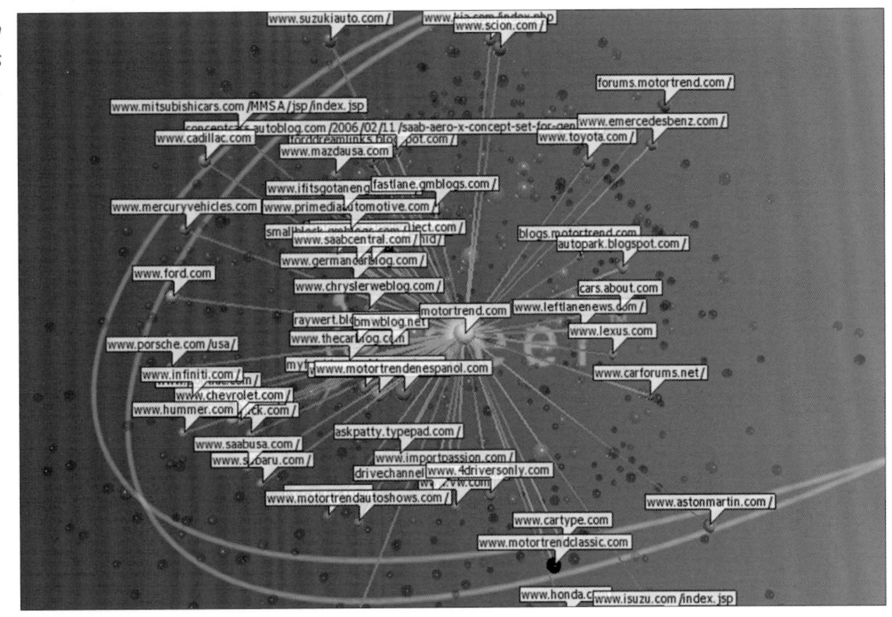

conventional media in countries where conventional media are strictly controlled.

- If you have a genuinely new product, be prepared for the shock of the new. A lot of people react negatively to genuinely new ideas online because they make them feel uncomfortable. 'All great truths begin as blasphemies.' said George Bernard Shaw. Not all marketers get this.

Most people find the act of thinking stressful. Don't force them to do it online.

So?

If you want to use word of mouth effectively, you have to use it carefully:

- Do not lie, speak only the truth. Because in the digital world of the 21st century the people who are thinking about checking into your hotel tonight are speaking to the people who checked out last night.
- Make your message *simple.* Complex messages get lost in translation. Only simple messages get transmitted by users.
- Don't force consumers to *think*. Most consumers spend their lives avoiding having to think. People listen to music on their iPod because it takes one click to do so. They still watch analog TV because it takes one click to do so. They shop at Amazon because one-click ordering means you can buy without thinking.
- Above all, be *clear.* The digital world is far too complex for most consumers.

3. MARKETING IS ABOUT GETTING PEOPLE TO DO THINGS

Marketers are all about getting people to *think* things, in order for them to *do* things.

They do this because that's the way analog media worked:

1. You showed people an ad
2. You hoped that they then thought differently about the product
3. You hoped they then might go out and buy it.

But it is weak psychology.

If you really want people to think differently, it is usually much more effective to get them to do something, and *watch their minds follow in line.*

It's how Gandhi did it

In the 1930s, Indian nationalists had been making speeches against British rule for decades – without any impact.

So instead of using words, Gandhi decided to get Indians to *do* something instead.

He encouraged them to go to the seashore and make salt.

Salt was essential to human life in a hot country like India.

But because the British government controlled the making of salt, anyone else who made salt was breaking the law.

So when Gandhi's followers arrived at the seashore, British soldiers beat them.

They did so in front of the world media.

Public opinion changed. And a few years later, the British left India.

It works today too

Successful consumer campaigns today follow the same thinking:

- If you want car drivers to support your cause, you ask them to *honk for peace.*
- If you want people to support breast cancer awareness, you ask them to *wear a pink bow.*
- If you want a captive released, you *tie a yellow ribbon around a tree.*

Digital media are all interactive. All let you ask people to respond and commit.

In March 1519, Hernando Cortez landed in Mexico with five hundred Spanish troops.

His orders were to conquer the Aztec empire.

But he faced a morale problem.

Cortez wanted to march inland and take the Aztec capital.

But his troops feared the armies awaiting them.

They wanted to sail back to their girlfriends in Cuba.

Cortez wondered what to do.

Had he been a classical marketer, he might have put up some posters around his camp saying:

THE SPANISH EMPIRE NEEDS YOU

Or perhaps from focus groups he might have identified the key barrier in his men's minds, and addressed it with:

HEY, THE AZTECS AREN'T REALLY THAT SCARY

Or if he'd had a direct marketing background, he might have tried:

KILL 20 AZTECS AND WIN A GOLD COIN

But Cortez knew a little more about human motivation than most marketers.

He knew that for humans, attitudes and beliefs are not absolute, they are a function of what they do.

Cortez's men were unsure about continuing his mission because they had the option not to do so.

And so Cortez decided to remove that option.

He went down to the bay where the Spanish fleet was moored.

And he burned their boats.

What happened next?

Initially, his men were shocked.

Some were mutinous.

But faced with no option but to go on, they rapidly regained their motivation.

The result: Cortez's force of five hundred Spaniards took on the Aztec empire – and won.

500 years later

Meanwhile today, the world's greatest corporations spend billions of dollars trying to appeal to our reason and emotion.

They do not always get a return.

But hidden in their market research is Cortez's learning – that making people *do* things in order to make them *think* things can be more effective than the other way round.

So as the lead medium changes from TV to digital, marketers need to stop worrying about how to persuade people to *think* things, and ask them to *do* things instead.

Digital marketers should ponder the gentle words of Lyndon B. Johnston: 'Get them by the balls, and their hearts and minds will follow.'

So:

1. When young people on MySpace or FaceBook want to start a trend, they invite their friends to join a network, like 'Jessica Alba or Jessica Biel?' or 'People who have to spell their names to other people'. Brand marketers need to follow the same logic – allowing people to join their groups (and to do so with one click, rather than having to enter a pageful of information.)
2. In the analog era, persuading customers to recruit their friends and family for a brand was difficult, because it involved filling in and processing coupons. In the digital era though, tasking brand ambassadors is easy. Ask them to do things - *and then reward them for doing so.*
3. Why ask people to go out and try a digital product, when digital media can give them a sample? Getting people to experience the first few levels of a computer game is much more powerful marketing than asking people to think about a benefit.

   In the TV era, getting trial happened at the end of the marketing process. Today, it should often be the *start.*

4. WATCH WHAT HAPPENS AFTER THE CLICK

Joe Smith wants a new camera.

A friend told him a new one called the TM-1 is cool.

Joe looks it up on a search engine.

Joe types 'TM-1' into the search box and presses return.

The search engine goes into action.

Wizzzz

Within 0.03 seconds it finds all the 67,000 pages on the web with TM-1 in them.

Within those 0.03 seconds it also orders those 67,000 pages by their importance, and displays the ten most influential results.

It then looks through its list of advertisers, sees which ones have asked for TM-1 as a search term, picks the most popular ads above a certain price, ranks them by popularity, and places them on the search page.

All within the same 0.03 seconds.

Joe Smith looks at the page.

His eye is caught by one of the text-based ads about the TM-1's revolutionary new features.

'12 megapixel pocket-sized camera!' says the link.

'Wow!' thinks Joe.

'I want one!'

And he clicks on it.

In total, no more than three seconds have passed since Joe pressed 'search'.

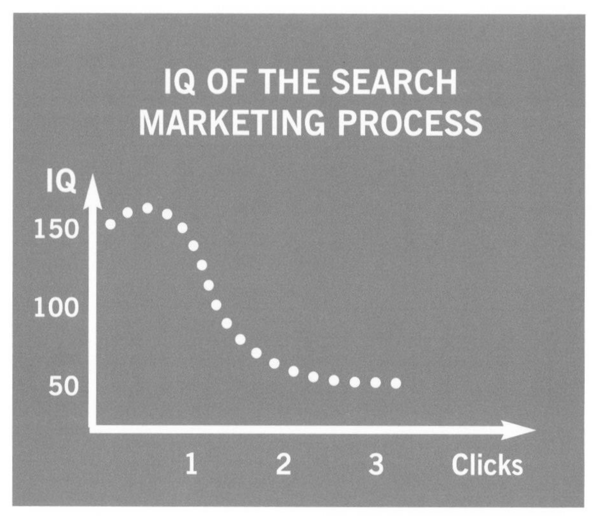

Search marketing is really smart - until the user hits the landing page.

But then...

Joe's experience so far is state-of-the-art 21st century use of computers.

But now things change.

Up comes the camera company's home page.

Joe looks at the page, and finds nothing about the TM-1.

He looks at the links on the page and wonders which one to click.

The choices include 'corporate social responsibility', 'investor relations' and 'enterprise-level solutions.'

Joe is confused.

'It's great that this company is single-handedly saving the planet,' he thinks.

'And it's wonderful that it is fully compliant with Sarbanes Oxley.'

'And I'm sure someone must be interested in its stellar track record in industrial components.'

'But what I want to know about is the TM-1, already!'

Joe sees a search box on the company's website. He types 'TM-1' into it.

He draws a blank.

So he types in 'consumer digital cameras' and is sent to the company's brochure download page.

Eventually, Joe finds some stuff about cameras in the brochures.

Joe clicks on a link, spends a minute downloading a PDF file.

But the camera company's print production people sent this year's brochure to the printers before the TM-1 was announced.

So its PDF contains nothing about the TM-1.

Joe gives up

Joe gives up and tries another link from the search engine's homepage.

It's a consumer camera review site.

As the TM-1 is new, there is only one review.

It's from a thirteen year old in Bakersfield.

'The TM-1 is shit.' states the thirteen year old definitively.

He hates his TM-1 because he wanted his pop to buy him a more expensive camera.

Joe pauses. 'I guess the TM-1 is not as good as it's said to be.' he thinks.

And so the sale of the TM-1 fails.

Because the massive multinational consumer electronics company didn't use the web as smartly as the thirteen year old from Bakersfield.

Not uncommon

This scenario happens millions of times a day on the web at the moment.

Indeed 96% of clicks lead to absolutely nothing.

Simply because the quality of thinking and computing that happens *after* the click is minimal compared with the amount of computing intelligence that happens *before* the click.

If search-led digital commerce is ever going to reach its potential, we need to put a lot more thinking into what happens after the user clicks.

Why do so many website structures reflect corporate organograms?

After the click

That's why Wunderman has developed a new line of thinking called 'After the Click'.

Its basic principles are as follows:

- Unless it has been demonstrated otherwise, each search term needs its own landing page. People searching for 'lcd tv' don't want to find refrigerators on the page they land on.
- The thinking on your landing page should reflect the promise in your pay-per-click ad. If your pay-per-click ad promises low, low prices, your landing

page should focus on low, low prices, not on service agreements.

- People who click on pay-per-click ads are already interested in what you have to sell. Don't bother persuading them that they want a new DVD player. Just persuade them that your DVD player is what they need (and that you can get it into their hands fast, cheaply and securely).
- Search engines do well because they put the entire web a click away. So don't force people to click repeatedly through your site to get to the information you've advertised.
- Consumer landing pages should not contain links to your corporate information. Investors and analysts need their own investor relations website. *A website that talks to everyone talks to no one.*
- Keep checking that what you are doing is working. *'It's wonderful to have a good strategy,'* said Winston Churchill. *'But one should occasionally have a look at the results.'*

The consumer doesn't care whether you're Sarbanes-Oxley compliant or not.

5. KEEPING PEOPLE WAITING IS A SIN

Back in 1997, download speeds were around one hundred times slower than they are today.

Pictures downloaded like this:

Then like this:

Then like this:

Internet entrepreneurs like Jeff Bezos realised that consumers didn't like waiting ages for their page to load.

He made the Amazon homepage out of text - because text loaded instantly.

So did Filo and Yang when they set up Yahoo.

So did Matt Drudge when he set up the Drudge Report.

Boo.com launched a flash-based fashion retail site in 1997, in the days before most people had the Flash plug-in on their browsers.

Not surprisingly, no one bought anything.

Meanwhile

Meanwhile web designers, agencies and marketers decided that this wasn't the right approach.

They decided instead that what mattered were brand values, and that meant big, graphics-rich sites which downloaded at a snail's pace.

Other brand marketers went further and insisted that consumers had to be motivated enough to download an obscure plug-in to their web browser before they could enjoy their exciting sales copy.

Not surprisingly, the consumer learned to give brand sites a miss, and stick to the editorial.

Today though

In today's broadband world, download speeds are a thousand times faster than in 1997.

Graphics-rich sites load instantly.

So internet entrepreneurs like Chris DeWolfe have allowed pages on MySpace to contain lots of graphics.

And highly compressed video also plays instantly, leading to the success of YouTube.

Meanwhile, from brand websites you get:

LOADING

And then after a while, you get:

LOADING

And eventually, if you can be bothered to remain there long enough, you get:

LOADING

About half a website's audience moves on if it doesn't load within ten seconds.

Brand marketers have repeated their mistake.

So

So, if the web is to work for marketers, they need to appreciate bandwidth:

1. People visit the web to read stuff that is interesting, and marketing sometimes manages to hitch a ride. Marketing needs to load *faster* than the editorial, not slower.
2. Slow loading websites may look cool in a presentation (where the website has been stored on the laptop's hard drive), but they cause visitors to desert in droves. *You can't save souls in an empty church.*

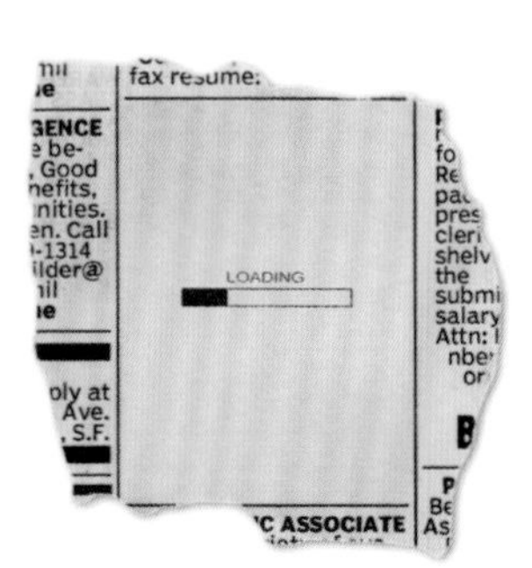

Thank goodness analog ads don't work like some brand websites.

3. Don't blame the technology: Flash-based sites can load instantly – if you design your experience so that you don't need big graphics and movie files until later in your timeline.
4. Don't worry so much about production values. The most effective ads on the world wide web are Google's text-based adlinks – with production values close to zero.
5. Take your quality cues from editorial on the web. 'The best advertising' said advertising creatives 40 years ago 'looks like editorial'. The same is true today. Sponsored links work well because they look like editorial, not ads.
6. Similarly, LonelyGirl15.com took off on the web because a huge number of people thought that hers was a genuine videoblog by a repressed 15 year old. Like the Blair Witch Project, things have much more impact if you *think they are for real.*

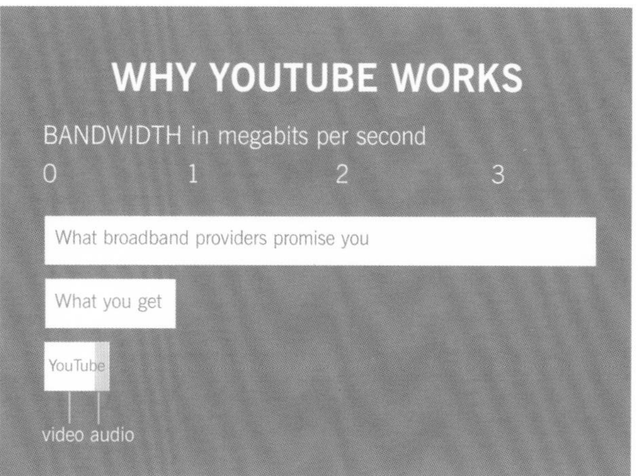

6. YOU'RE A DATAPHOBE. GET OVER IT

Most marketers went into marketing rather than finance because they liked ideas, not numbers.

Digital is full of 'metrics' and 'ratios' and other things with numbers in them. So they are scared of it.

Marketers need to get their heads around digital.

But they are right to be cautious about numbers in large quantities.

In the past, gushing digital data streams have *killed* marketing departments.

Back in 1988

Back in 1988, every supermarket chain in the US and Europe introduced barcode scanners at their checkouts.

Their marketing departments then set out to analyze the data and turn it into consumer insights.

But the more they looked at it, the bigger the task grew.

And as this happened, the barcode data grew from megabytes to terabytes, and from terabytes to petabytes.

Twenty years later, most of these marketing departments (with the notable exceptions of Kroger in the United States and Britain's Tesco) have yet to find a single consumer insight in their data.

Today, the data is like a vast river gushing into their marketing departments, demanding more and more storage and more and more attention.

It's a classic case of paralysis through analysis.

So

It's clear that if you want consumer insights out of data, *you need to know where to look.*

To do this, you may need specialist help.

As the Wunderman Network's analytics partner ZAAZ.com in Seattle puts it:

1. The first step is to make sure that the data you are looking at is accurate. False indicators have sometimes convinced companies that their website traffic is *four* times its true value.
2. One percent of the data holds ninety-nine percent of the insights. The trick is to find the right one percent.
3. The right one percent may not lie in clickstreams at all. As ZAAZ found when working on Converse boots, the insights lay not in clickstreams, but in the *search terms* site users used. Everyone thought they navigated the Converse site looking for shoe models and styles. But analysis of customer search

When people search the Converse boots website, they search as much for colors as they do for models and styles.

patterns revealed that half the visitors were just searching for 'black' or 'red' or 'green' shoes. *This knowledge helped Converse restructure their site, and raise visitors and sales substantially.*

4. Data should not be relied on in isolation. In ZAAZ's hi-tech usability lab, website testers reveal problems, ambiguities and confusions that clickstreams do not.
5. Be careful to observe actual behavior, rather than assume what happens. When mobile phone companies set up wap portals 2003/4, they put news headlines on the opening page because analog newspapers put news headlines on their front pages. If they had looked closer, they would have noticed that most of the young men they were appealing to started reading their analog newspaper on the *back page,* where the sports headlines and scores are.

   Four years and a billion dollars of investment later, most mobile portals now open with the sports news and scores first.
6. Be aware that the act of measurement itself can change your traffic flows. Many brochureware sites involve elaborate navigation before your visitors get to download your brochure pdfs. The elaborate navigation causes many users not to bother.
7. Above all, think carefully about whether you are right to ask people for personal details before you allow them into your website. Any bricks and mortar shop that behaved in this way would go out of business. Excessive demand for customer details

No real-world store would do this, but plenty of websites do.

is one of the biggest destroyer of website effectiveness there is.

8. The websites that are organised like corporate departments - with investor relations, environmental policies and business-to-business links mixed in with the consumer product offer annoy and confuse consumers more than any other.
9. There's a big difference between technology that definitely works and technology that pretty much works. In Europe and Asia, an SMS text is pretty much guaranteed to reach its intended recipient, and so SMS is a standard means of communication.

   In the US though, no one can be 100% sure that their text will migrate from network to network, and therefore text volumes lie way below those in Europe.

   Similarly, whilst many e-tailers worry about abandoned shopping baskets in their stores, few are willing to admit that the reason for the abandoned trolleys is a feeling amongst shoppers that their money and purchases are not quite 100% secure.
10. Most companies have separate brand divisions that run separate websites, separate analytics and separate financials. But often it is the way a customer moves from site to site within the company's products that matters. If your company has several divisions, *make sure the network between them works.*

Most young men start reading newspapers from the back – because that's where the sports news is.

Mobile phone portals now open sports first too.

11. If you are in corporate management, be careful about setting *ratios* as targets. If you bonus your web marketers on their ability to increase the proportion of your website visitors who buy, some website designers will set out improve your e-commerce experience. But others will set out to discourage casual traffic from entering your site. *This latter group is more likely to hit their bonus.*

    In some countries, hospital managers are often rewarded by the proportion of their callers who get dealt with within 24 hours.
    This is supposed to motivate them to process more patients per day
    But many have realized that they can achieve the same result by making it more difficult for people to get on to the waiting list in the first place.

    Today, many websites boast a high conversion rate from visitors to prospects because only the most committed visitors will wait the 30 seconds for a website to load.

    Management by ratio can kill a website.

ZAAZ's book Actionable Web Analytics is available from Amazon.

7. DON'T WAIT FOR THE DUST TO SETTLE

Talk to many marketing executives about why they haven't made a move to digital, and they will explain that the media aren't ready yet.

Whilst television is polished and professional, social networking sites and other digital media are anarchic and uncontrolled.

They are waiting until digital settles down into as tried and trusted a medium as television and newspapers have been for the past fifty years.

They will have a long wait.

Because the digitization of media is driven by Moore's Law.

Moore's Law, first defined by Gordon Moore of Intel in 1967, says that the power of computers doubles every eighteen months.

Moore's Law continues to operate today.

And all parties involved agree that Moore's Law will continue to operate for the next twenty years.

Coming soon, for your 100 megapixel pocket camera.

WEB 2.0 STRATEGIC FRIDGE MAGNETS

Instructions: *1. Stick this page to adhesive magnetic card.*
2. Cut out words 3. Rearrange into a Web 2.0 strategy.
4. Call a venture capitalist.

folksonomic | digital space | wiki | a | streaming | UGC

and | long tail | achieve | social networking | vertical | MySpacer

monetize | SSL | avatar | virtual | bricks to clicks | -plex | long tail

ergonomic | deanalogize | justify | podcast | distributed | wisdom

MP4 | set top box | but | holistic | wrap-round | flash memory

terabyte | T3 | 380bps | pay-per-action | early adopter | lonelygirl

hope to | usercentric | community | surround-sound | VGA | p.p.c.

we | wom | vodcast | multiple play | cyber | 3.0 | Moore's Law

scalable | intuitive | create | piped | M4V | partnership | broadband

gamer-friendly | console | experiential | 720p | democratic

HDMI | crowdsource | MP3 | white hat | firewall | serverfarm

strategic | develop | megapixel | 1080i | media-rich

parameter | metrics | user-tested | define | measurable

thus | herdthink | predict | in order to

In the last fifteen years, computers have become 100 times faster. They will become 100 times faster and more powerful in the next fifteen years too.

Put simply, digital marketing *will continue to evolve at breakneck speeds for the rest of your career.*

The dust isn't going to settle for *two decades* yet.

Panic now

This huge uncertainty means that media planning is becoming as experimental and as uncertain as creative content has been in the past.

Even relatively established digital media are in reality just works in progress.

Take the plasma display panels that have been appearing in shops across the world for the past few years.

There is no agreed upon theory of how to use them:

- Airports use plasma panels as *media of information.*
- Supermarkets are trying to use them as *in-store television.* At the time of writing, supermarket television is not doing as well as the supermarkets had hoped, as shoppers tend not to notice, or indeed want to watch television pictures flashing above their heads.
- Other media companies are now trying to use them as *highly localized* advertising media in burger bars and other locations.
- Wander around Toy'R'Us Times Square branch, and you'll see plasma panels used for *quizzes.*

The main people who look at supermarket TV are the same as those who look at the giant promotional floor stickers – kids.

Perhaps if supermarkets put the plasma screens on the fronts of the carts they might get more impact amongst moms.

And if the carts had GPS, so they knew which aisle they were in, we'd have a really smart medium.

- Go to the fashionable Spoon restaurant in Budapest, and all the framed *old master paintings* on the walls change every 30 seconds – because the pictures in the frames are actually plasma display panels.

Everyone is learning as they go.

Marketers need to adopt this 'permanent beta' mentality if they are going to survive:

1. Get ready to fail

In the TV era, you could produce the crappiest TV commercial in the world, and you could still present your media buying report to your board and point out that you had achieved 100 million impacts.

In the digital era, you can create the greatest website in the world, and still get no hits.

Marketers, and agencies, need to get used to living with *frequent and very public humiliations.*

2. Stay alert

The continuous innovation in media that will happen over the next twenty years means that no one's marketing strategy is likely to be bullet proof for more than a couple of years.

Most companies need to live with a *heightened sense of competitive threat.*

Resisting threats means constantly reviewing marketing strategies, rethinking assumptions and constantly testing new routes.

For marketers who have built their careers on their

Most companies need to live with a heightened sense of competitive threat.

To check out video billboards and other emerging media, take a walk along Shanghai's Nanjing Lu and Huaihai Lu.

ability to spend big budgets without controversy, this is likely to be an entirely new world.

3. The biggest threat is to the biggest brands

The cost of a TV campaign was the biggest factor barring new entrants from entering markets for most of the late 20th century.

Most of the costs of launching a new brand were variable: to produce ten million pots of jam, it took ten times as many labels, jars and lids and ten times as much jam as it did to produce one million pots of jam.

But it cost the same to run a heavyweight TV campaign for your ten million pots of jam as it did for your one million pots of jam.

The end result was that the ten million pot brand made all the money, and the one million pot brand didn't make a profit at all.

All that is now gone.

Most big startups today, from Google to Starbucks, spend very little money on TV to establish themselves.

In our connected world, they do it instead by strategic partnerships, by word of mouth and by other, cheaper media.

The marketing economies of scale that made many big brands secure businesses have *evaporated.*

4. The threat is from niches

Similarly, businesses that talk to small, deep audiences have had a huge boost from new media.

Ten years ago it was impossible to build a business in a highly niche area, because the potential of the

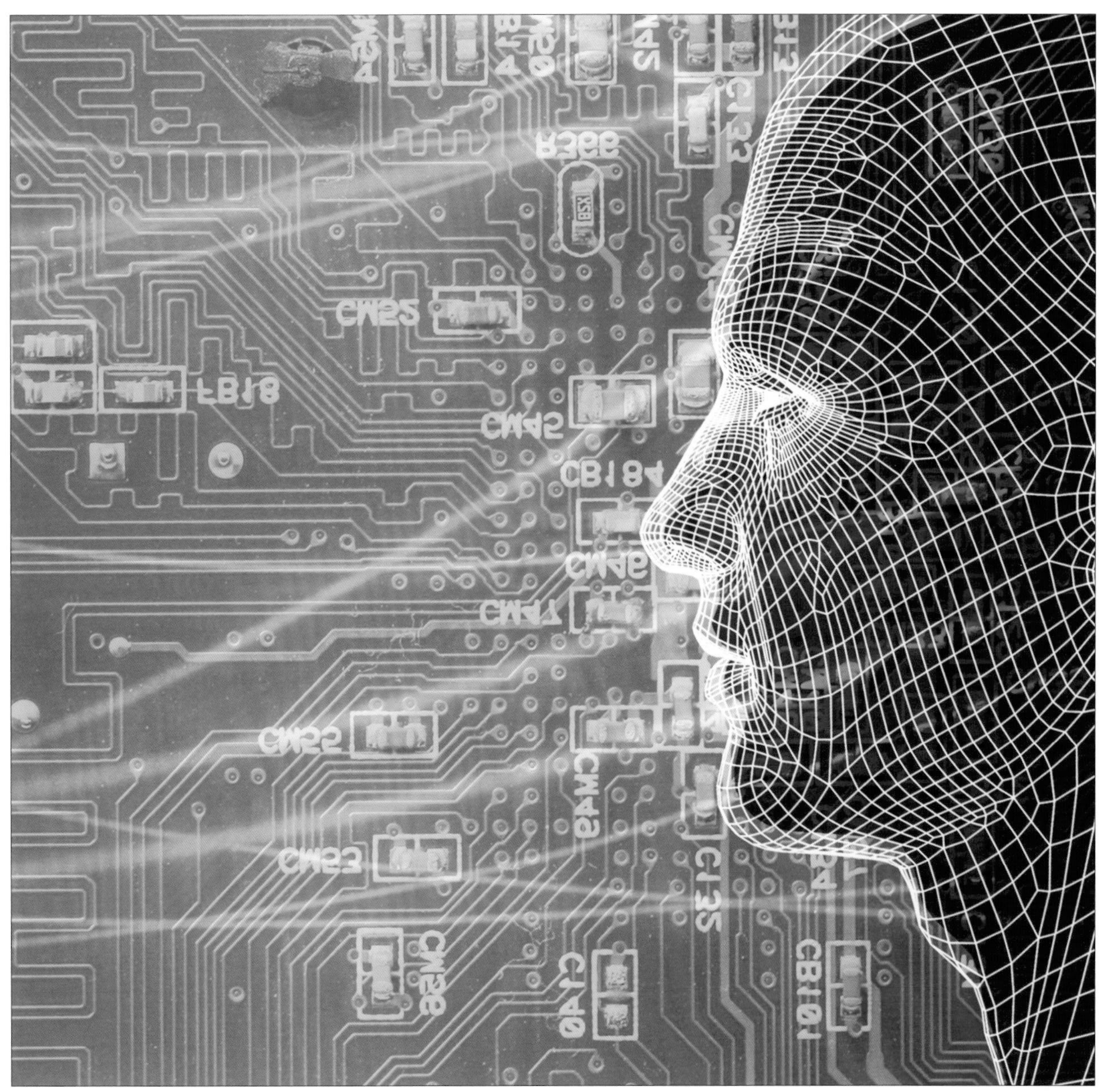

By 2040, the intellectual capacity of a $1,000 computer is likely to exceed that of the human race. The day when computers acquire consciousness and choose no longer to be the servants of mankind may be inevitable.

business never exceeded the media cost of launching it.

Today, people selling a book with a market of no more than 1000 readers can do so profitably via Amazon, and someone selling music from a rock band with no fans outside of Fresno can do so profitably via iTunes.

These niche businesses can become big: a niche Austrian site trading plastic discs called Tazos became eBay.

In the past, big brands felt secure because they knew that they had covered all viable niches and segments in their market.

Today, they can no longer be sure.

Today's top-of-the-range iPod has space for 2,000 CDs worth of songs – more than most people will ever buy.

But within a few years, the capacity of iPods will be enough to store every piece of music ever recorded in the history of mankind.

5. Think *biological*

If you decide to travel in rural tropical areas, your doctor will tell you to take malaria pills.

But the pills he tells you to take this year will be *different* to the ones he told you to take two years ago.

That's because it only takes two years for the mosquito population in a particular area to become immune to mankind's defenses, and to pose a new health threat.

It's the same with digital marketing. A few years ago, everyone used e-mail marketing, as a more effective and cheaper form of communication than traditional direct mail. Then spam blockers appeared, and then email programs stopped displaying graphic email content from unrecognized senders, and suddenly e-mail marketing is a lot less effective than it was before.

Marketers must act like doctors, *evolving their plans rapidly as the ecosystem fights back.*

8. A RELATIONSHIP CAN LAST A LIFETIME

In a business where you can lose 40% of your customers each year, a mobile service provider who loses only five percent a year usually counts themselves as lucky.

But in Europe today everyone has a cellphone, the market is mature, and it is very difficult to get new customers in.

So five percent churn can mean a five percent smaller business each year. Within five years, a quarter of your business will be gone.

That five percent loss each year can be catastrophic.

But

But most of those people needn't be lost.

Wunderman research reveals that it's usually only *one* of the five percent are so angry at you that there is no way you can keep them.

The other four percent are people who would have stayed - if you'd asked them.

The LG 'Shine' phone's built-in mirror lets you check your looks as you check your texts.

How to ask them

Most mobile service providers argue that they already have huge, powerful loyalty schemes, rewarding people with points, plus wonderful mailings that land on their doorsteps every month with their bill.

But any mobile service provider who acts in this way is missing the point.

All the stuff they send and mail and text their customers is little more than spam at the time when they are not thinking of leaving.

And it isn't there at the time when they are thinking of leaving.

Put simply, most loyalty mailings don't hit the right people at the right time.

The two-week window

The time between a customer becoming dissatisfied, and their making a move to cancel their contract, is typically no more than two weeks.

Put another way, if you experience five percent churn each year, it is caused by no more than *one in five hundred* customers being dissatisfied at any one time.

Put another way, if you are sending out loyalty mailings to your entire customer base, 499 out of 500 of them are currently missing the mark.

Zeroing in

The fact is that most people thinking of dumping their

mobile contract send out very clear signals in the days before their decision.

If a mobile service provider picks up on these signals and acts on them instantly, most of the dissatisfied will stay.

Customer Lifetime Management

Of course, it's massively expensive and complex to do this using people. It has to be done through *software.*

And this is what has led Wunderman Denmark to put together the Customer Lifetime Management program:

- In the days before they make a decision to leave a mobile service provider, most customers send out signals.
- Perhaps their decision to defect is the result of a high bill. The program identifies people about to receive an *exceptionally high bill* and flags them for special handling.
- Another thing that causes people to defect is when their phone usage *drops.* Again, activity at the right time can hold on to them.
- Others defect because the way they use their phone changes. Say a woman starts a new relationship with a man where she texts him 30 times a day. She may suddenly be attracted by monthly airtime packages with 1000 free texts a month in a rival's store window.
- The moment a customer enters a high-risk category, they are served with relevant offers. A customer whose usage is rising is offered a better value plan. One whose usage is declining may be

HOW TO REALLY UPSET YOUR CUSTOMERS

'Sorry sir, we're having problems transferring your number to your new service provider.'

'Sorry madam, I'm not authorized to let you leave. You've got to talk to my supervisor, but he's in the rest room.'

'I know our dial-up software won't uninstall from your computer. It's to stop you canceling your subscription. Duuh.'

offered a lower line rental. One who starts texting heavily should be offered a 1000-texts-a-month package deal.

- Every nugget of knowledge gleaned from the customer over the years must be brought into play. If they have enquired about a family plan in the past, get talking about family plans.
- Those who do decide to leave should be thanked genuinely for their past custom, and allowed to leave without impediment. (There is nothing more upsetting to a disaffected customer than the tricks some phone, financial and utility companies play on their customers to prevent them leaving.)
- They should then be made motivating offers to try to keep them. (If the software finds out they are leaving because a rival provider has offered them a cheap Nokia 95, it offers them a cheap Nokia N95 to stay.)

Read more about relationship marketing at pubs.wunderman.com/spam.pdf

The program really works

Wunderman Denmark is implementing the customer lifetime management program in a number of countries.

Amongst customers within the program, churn can fall by 50%.

The approach can also save lives

The approach works in the area of medicine too.

When a cancer patient leaves hospital, they are not usually given the 'all clear' immediately.

In most cases, they have to keep taking pills for

several years to ensure that the cancer doesn't come back.

The trouble is, once they leave hospital, many patients feel better.

They want to forget about their experience, and get on with life.

So they stop taking their pills.

And, a few years later, the cancer comes back.

Wunderman, together with its healthcare partner Sudler and Hennessy have been working in this area too.

We have a history of creating support groups and compliance programs for a variety of patient types.

And we've worked on systems to ensure that the patients get timely SMS text reminders to keep taking their pills.

The systems help doctors and pharmaceutical companies ensure the best possible outcome for the patient.

A program of SMS texts can help patients to take the right pills at the right time.

9. HOW TO FIND THE PERFECT PARTNER

In the digital era, every brand is a media owner, and can grow through strategic partnerships.

In 1998, Google didn't exist.

Today it is valued at $168 billion, more than General Motors.

According to WPP's BrandZ study, it is the most powerful brand in the world.

Marketing was a vital part of Google's rise.

But Google got to number one without spending a single cent on traditional advertising.

Google did it entirely through *strategic partnerships.*

The first big one was with AOL.

The partnership put a Google search bar on the AOL homepage.

This put Google in front of 36 million web-literate Americans.

They tried Google.

And because they liked it, they told their friends.

Within a year or so, everyone knew about Google.

It was so famous, it became a verb.

AOL benefited too.

They had introduced their users to a cool new service, and their ratings improved in line.

BRANDZ GLOBAL TOP 10

		2006 value in $billion
1.	Google	66.4
2.	GE (General Electric)	61.9
3.	Microsoft	55.0
4.	Coca-Cola	44.1
5.	China Mobile	41.2
6.	Marlboro	39.2
7.	Wal-Mart	36.9
8.	Citi	33.7
9.	IBM	33.6
10.	Toyota	33.4

* Coca-Cola's value includes Coke and Diet Coke/Coke Light

Google became the world's most valuable brand in just seven years.

Häagen Dazs did it with Baileys

Many other companies have tried strategic partnerships, each brand using the other to extend its awareness, and to provoke new consumers to try it.

In the 90s, Diageo were very successful partnering two of their brands to produce Baileys flavor Häagen-Dazs.

The partnership produced a profitable brand extension.

It also made a lot of Häagen-Dazs users try Baileys, and vice versa.

When it works, the strategic partnership can be very effective: each brand benefits from rising awareness and a new group of potential new users. And because no media costs are involved, strategic partnerships can be cheap to run.

But it's not as easy as it looks

But many other strategic partnerships have failed.

There are many reasons for this, but the basic reason is that the brands didn't fit.

Couldn't the companies have checked this in advance?

The problem most companies face is that they have no research in this area - all their research is within their own category.

Should Coke partner with Nike?

All Coke's research is about soft drinks.

Should Nike partner with Coke?

All Nike's research is about sports apparel.

This is why Wunderman has developed its brand partnerships tool.

It's a scientific analysis tool, based on a Wunderman/Y&R survey called BrandAsset Valuator.

BrandAsset Valuator is a global survey of attitudes towards brands, based on interviews with 500,000 consumers using 30,000 brands.

BrandAsset Valuator is the perfect partnerships tool, because it ignores categories, and measures all brands in exactly the same way.

We use it to look at:

1: Shared DNA

Here we look at the two potential partners' 48 key brand attributes, and see what level of correlation there is between them.

Brands with a very high level of DNA in common score close to 1; brands with nothing in common score close to 0; brands with *contrary* DNA score negatively on the test. (Contrary DNA is revealed, for

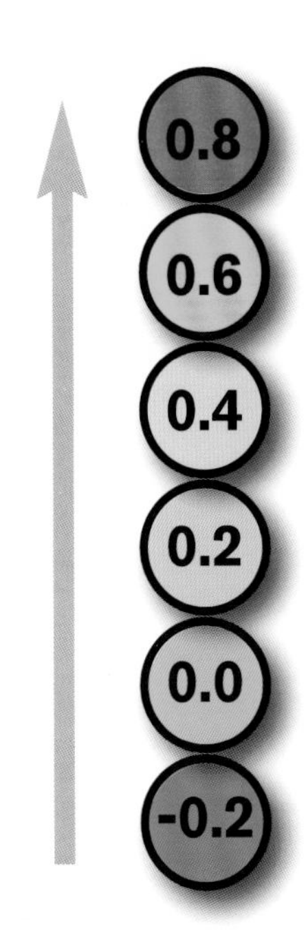

The shared DNA scale: a good partnership like Baileys and Häagen-Dazs scores around 0.8. A bad partnership scores 0.4 or below.

example when you try to partner a breakfast cereal with a drain cleaner.)

As a rule of thumb, we say that anything over 60% is fine. Anything below 40% and alarm bells ring.

2: Imagery exchange

When two people hook up together, a successful partnership benefits each of them – and does so in different ways.

When supermodel Kate Moss shacked up with BabyShambles front man Pete Doherty in 2005, both of their celebrity personas benefited:

- 33-year Kate made herself relevant to a new generation of teenage BabyShambles fans.
- Pete got BabyShambles exposed to a much wider audience than he could otherwise possibly have hoped.

It's the same with most other partnerships; what each half brings to the other is a vital part of the connection.

THE IMAGERY EXCHANGE MAP

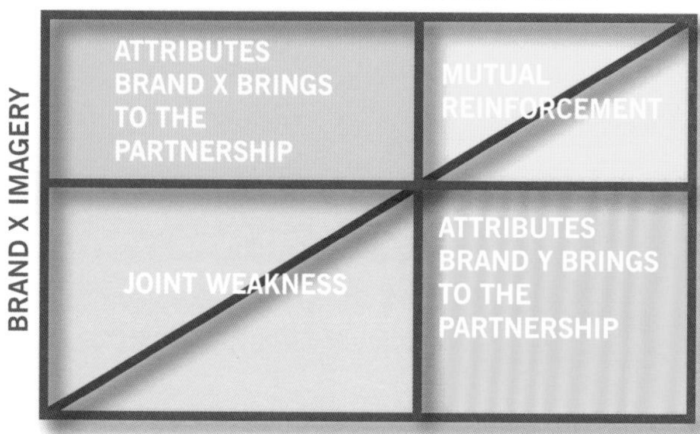

And so when we study two potential partner brands, we look at which brand attributes are shared and which are brought by one brand only to the party.

We plot these attributes on an 'imagery exchange' map.

On the map, attributes that lie in the green area are what Brand X brings to the partnership; attributes in the orange area are what Brand Y brings to the partnership; attributes that fall in the yellow area are already held strongly by both brands, and attributes that fall in the blue area are ones that both brands possess only weakly.

Analysis like this can *quantify precisely* what the partnership brings to each brand.

In Britain, supermarket Tesco partners with Esso service stations. But Tesco is increasingly the dominant brand, and in focus groups, people who previously referred to a site as 'Esso' now refer to it as 'Tesco'.

3: Assessing relative scale

Here's a question for the average guy.

Should you date Paris Hilton?

The answer is no, because:

- She wouldn't respect you.
- Her tastes would bankrupt you.
- All her friends would look down on you.

The central problem: Paris Hilton as a person and as a brand is in a much stronger position than you are.

This is why in our third test, we measure the relative positions of potential partners on a diagram called the BrandAsset Valuator PowerGrid.

Brands in a roughly similar position of strength can make good partnerships.

Those that are not need to think hard about how their relationship will work.

The diagnosis

The more partnership tests we do, the more definitive our recommendations become.

1. Partnerships can work where two brands are quite

Partnerships of equals can be very effective.

different, indeed the fact that the two brands are in very different markets means that each brand grows without cannibalizing the other's user base. But if the two brands have very little in common, better stay away. Opposites do not always attract.

2. Partnerships fail when one partner doesn't bring much to the table – either because it doesn't have much strength as a brand, or because it lacks positive brand attributes. If an insurance company asks to partner with you, *their check book had better be large.*
3. Beware brands that have 'traditional' as a large part of their brand image. This can damage your cool, trendy brand beyond measure. Partnerships with boring, traditional companies are slowly draining the lifeblood out of Yahoo.
4. Work on the *logic* of your partnership. A clear consumer story about why you are working together will make the partnership stick in the popular consciousness.
5. Be careful: a failed partnership can damage a brand for years.

Read more about the Wunderman Brand Partnerships Consultancy at http://pubs.wunderman.com/partner.pdf

10. THE CHANNEL OF WE

Over the past two years, social networking websites have gained hundreds of millions of users. They have become the operating system teens and twenty-somethings use to run their social lives.

And deservedly so:

1. Social networking sites let them check out friends of friends: the source of most people's dates.
2. Social networking sites tell them when those friends of friends are in relationships, and when they're not. *So they know exactly when to hit on them.*
3. Many teens struggle with email because email demands grammar whereas their vocabulary extends to just 'hey', 'duuh' and 'whatever'. Social networking sites allow them to connect without having to write prose.
4. Social networking sites let young men check out their mates' biggest secret: their attractive younger sister. On spring break. In her bikini.

Tomorrow's megastars are today promoting themselves on MySpace.

5. Social networking builds village-like communities within cities, colleges and companies.
6. Microblogging features on sites like Twitter.com allow people to keep their close circle of friends informed of their every move and thought.
7. Social networking sites let them effortlessly share last night's photos with friends.
8. And to point out whose tongue was down whose throat.
9. Social networking also gives them direct access to their favorite celebrities, free from the jaded filter of journalism. Many journalists thought Paris deserved to go to jail. *Now you can hear her side.*

10 Social networking sites also let musicians build a fanbase for their rock band or rap MC.

11 And through partnerships with iTunes, social networking sites now allow those bands to sell music direct to their fans, cutting out the conventional record company.

12 Professional social networks like Linkedin.com offer jobs, contacts and references.

13 Above all, in countries where people access the web via their office computers, social networking provides a stimulating *alternative to working.*

Social networking has thus become a killer app of the world wide web.

'WELCOME TO THE WORLD OF TIMEWASTING.'

OFFICE WORKER,
EUROPE 2007

But marketers struggle to use it

But marketers struggle to use social networking. When they do so, they do so clumsily, using broad demographics to place marketing materials all over the site.

Social networkers may tolerate dumb advertising on TV, but when it appears on 'their' space, they move on. This is one reason why people are migrating from MySpace to Facebook.

And FaceBook too is now surrendering to commercial imperatives, as ads from credit reference agencies start to appear in FaceBook newsfeeds.

Marketers need to think harder:

MySpace started by recruiting L.A.'s surfers, models and musicians. The rest of the world followed.

1. All people on the sites are not the same

Marketers who use broad demographic targeting on social networking sites are assuming that all 18-24s are the same.

But that was not the way the sites built themselves up.

- The founders of MySpace invited Los Angeles' communities of rock musicians, models and surfers to be their first MySpacers. And because where models, rock stars and surfers go, others follow, MySpace rapidly became the *biggest* social networking site.
- Similarly, FaceBook talked first exclusively to kids at

Chatrooms aren't much fun if you're the only person there.

Smartphones are giving social networking an extra edge. If you meet someone new in a nightclub, you don't want to wait until tomorrow to check out their profile.

college. And then when they opened the site up, millions of others followed.

- Also, in Korea, the SK Telecom CyWorld portal started by attracting sociable young women, knowing that where sociable young women go, men follow like flies. Cyworld now boasts almost 99% penetration amongst young Koreans.

Marketers should follow suit, introducing their cool new wares to the cooler people on social networking sites, and allowing them to introduce the wares to their friends and acolytes.

Vietnamese Texan rapper Tila Tequila emailed her 70,000 strong male fanbase and asking them to become her friend on MySpace.

Tila rapidly became the most popular person on MySpace and started appearing on chat shows.

2. Don't think individuals, think herds

Man likes to tell himself that he is a free-thinking individual, but in reality, as author Mark Earls argues in *Herds,* most of his behavior is that of a herd-based animal:

- When buying in a new market for the first time, research shows that most people gravitate towards buying the brand leader – *the one most other people buy.*
- Restaurants typically encourage their first diners of the day to sit at the table by the window because potential customers are attracted by the knowledge that *other people are already dining there.*
- And Wunderman's 4Cs consumer segmentation reveals that 'innovators' – people who decide themselves to do something, independent of others - are rare. There are many more 'early adopters' – people who wait for cool people to do something, and then copy them.

What kind of person are you? Take Wunderman's online 4Cs test at http://pubs.wunderman.com/4cs to find out.

Marketers should recognize and reflect these herd patterns when they use social networking.

Don't invite individual MySpacers to try out your new bar or restaurant: *invite groups of friends.*

Don't invite individuals to enter your competition either: invite groups of friends to *compete or collaborate* to win.

3. Social networking can communicate popularity

As Lindsay Lohan films like *Mean Girls* accurately reflect, your status at high school depends not on how clever you are, or how hard-working, but on how *popular* you are.

For many people, popularity is a key part of social networking. One of the most popular features on social networking sites is the counter that tells teens how many friends they have. For many teens, managing their popularity rating has become an end in its own right.

Popularity is just as important in the business world: business networking portal Linkedin.com finds executives competing to accumulate *more contacts than their colleagues.*

A sense of popularity is vital to many brands too.

In the TV era, brewers briefed their ad agencies to fill their beer commercials with people, because their research said that a beer that was perceived to be popular was likely to succeed.

In the online era though, many brands have tried to communicate popularity and have failed.

In the late 1990s, many spirits brands created online

Economists have observed a strong negative correlation between the speed of economic growth in a country and the length of women's skirts.

The 15-20% monthly growth in the SecondLife economy may explain the extraordinarily skimpy outfits many SecondLife users choose for their avatars.

social spaces where their users could interact. But few people bothered to download the software that allowed them to do so. *The spirits companies threw parties, and no one came.*

In the real world, only sad people go to a bar just for a drink. Most people want to socialize, perhaps meet a partner, and drink as they do so.

The same goes for web presences. Only a sad person goes to a website to drink in the brand values of a spirits brand. Drinks brands that aspire to be sociable need to give people *other reasons* to go there.

Research indicates that in some virtual worlds, as many as 19% of the women you meet are actually men.

4. The sites may be global, but the people on them are not

On SecondLife, Europeans and Americans don't mix much, because the Europeans go to bed before Americans get home from work.

And even the Europeans don't mix much – SecondLife is full of separate groups of Germans, Dutch, Spanish and Italians who don't mix because they don't speak each other's language.

On social networking sites, most people's friends are not just within the same country. They are within the same city.

Marketers should thus look at social networking as a *city-by-city* phenomenon rather than at broad, national demographics.

The web may be world wide, but its users are not.

11. EXPERIENCE IS WHAT MATTERS

In a traditional laboratory experiment there is a cage with two levers in it:

- The red lever dispenses a pellet of food when it is pushed.
- The blue lever does nothing.

If a few humans are then put into the cage and left there for a week, an interesting effect occurs.

What happens?

After a while, the humans will press the red lever whenever they are hungry.

And they will completely ignore the blue lever.

If you then drop a market researcher into the cage, the researcher can learn about their experience.

When the market researcher questions the humans, the humans are likely to tell the researcher that they associate the red lever with statements like, 'tasty/delicious food' and 'the sort of lever I prefer'.

If the humans were sophisticated, they might also agree with statements that the red lever was 'a lever for people like them' and 'part of a positive lifestyle.'

AIR TRAVEL HELL

Today, passengers spend much more time getting to the airport, queuing, being searched, waiting, and sitting in the plane on the ground waiting for a take-off slot or gate than they do in the air.

As post-9/11 air travel gets less and less pleasant, there is a tendency for airlines to blame all their problems on airport management, hoping that the passengers will absolve the airline of responsibility for the delays, broken gates and incompetent baggage handling. *That's not the way their consumer thinks.*

Here's some questions airline market researchers ought to be asking:

- Did you find the home hub airport we are so proud of 'pleasant' – or an 'overcrowded filthy hell hole'?
- Was the queue at security 'long' or 'very long'?
- Did you tolerate customer service behavior from airline employees that you would not tolerate anywhere else because of the *risk of a cavity search?*

And for business travelers:

- Did your frequent flyer status help speed your journey in any way whatsoever?
- Was the 'fast track' lane faster than the regular lane? Or was it *slower?*
- Was the frequent flyer lounge jammed full or merely 'over capacity'?
- Does the digitally driven frequent flyer scheme you are part of have any connection whatsoever to the analog travel experience you just went through?
- Or is the frequent flyer scheme operating *on a separate planet?*

The airline experience starts the moment you leave home. And every experience – positive and negative - you have until you reach your destination counts towards the airline brand experience, and therefore to the airline brand.

In short, the red lever would have built up all the aspects of a strong, positive brand personality.

And without the humans having been exposed to any television advertising whatsoever.

This is fundamental to digital marketing.

The most powerful driver of brand image and purchase intent is not television.

It is *experience.*

Brand image without TV

Most marketers struggle with the concept of experience though because it can't be broken down into small pieces and analysed.

Experience is *indivisible:*

- Apple succeeded with the iPod because it recognized that user experience is indivisible. Its iTunes software imports CDs, searches for track names on a database, labels the tracks, and loads them on to an iPod all with just one click.
- Similarly, Sir Richard Branson built up an enviable position in business class travel by recognizing that the plane journey starts as you leave your front door, and doesn't end until you open the front door at your destination.

  Virgin Atlantic placed limousines at the disposal of passengers at both ends of the journey, and ensured that passport and ticketing was done whilst the passenger sat, relaxed, in their limo.

So

Online, the positive experience we deliver must be the

When you first came across your favorite coffee shop, you coveted its products.

Those beautiful creamy cappuccinos; those smooth lattes; those zingy expresso shots.

You grew used to hugging the cup; the feel of the cardboard insulator, snuggling into leather sofas in the shop as you drank it.

And then the coffee company got greedy.

They decided to get even more revenue by putting a branded coffee machine in your office.

And you went to that machine.

And put a paper cup under it.

And pressed the dispense button.

But there were no cardboard insulators.

And so when you picked the cup up it burned you.

And the milk in your office fridge wasn't quite fresh.

So the beverage didn't taste as nice as it had done before.

And then you realized that the stuff in the cup was just coffee.

No different than the jar of granules in your kitchen.

And the brand experience you were in love with started to fade.

You can't deliver a great brand experience in one division, and deliver a poor one from another division, and expect the consumer to keep the two separate.

Brand experience is *indivisible.*

It's about everything you do.

total experience the prospect receives from the moment they think about their need.

1. There is no point having a slick website if it takes twenty five clicks for the prospect to find it. Or if the promises made in paid-for clicks don't match the content of the website. Or if the prospect can't find it at all.
2. The digital parts of the brand experience must work together with the analog parts. There is no point in having a cutting-edge digital frequent-flyer scheme, if your best customers still struggle to get through the airport.
3. If you sell everything under one house brand, the *whole* experience of your company is what matters. Ensure that all of your web presences work together.

The consumer doesn't care whether your business units are financially separate or not. All your web presences must work together.

12. IF YOU'VE GOT NOTHING TO HIDE, IT'S NOT A PROBLEM, RIGHT?

Digitization, argue civil libertarians, is making privacy the defining issue of the early 21st century.

And they are right:

- Commuters in London, England worry that their images are captured on closed circuit television *over 200 times a day.*
- Some South East Asian nations have linked their tax computers to their border control computers. So any expat who doesn't pay their taxes on time *doesn't get to go home for Christmas.*
- Jeans manufacturers in the US had to withdraw a plan to sew stock-control radio frequency ID tags into their seams because their wearers were *readily trackable* as they walked around the streets.

When Finns use their mobile phone to call the police, the police computer already knows where they are.

- Supermarkets worry about recruiting new mothers into their baby clubs: should they wait until the mother signs up before contacting her with baby related offers – *or can they identify pregnant shoppers from their folic acid purchases and write to them then?*
- And if they are doing that, why not identify potential mothers-to-be even earlier when they *stop buying condoms?*

Consumer concerns about privacy are heightened by the very real fears they have about ID theft. The best-selling durable item in upscale neighborhoods is not the wireless network, the iPhone or the Wii. It's the *cross-cut shredder.*

Many consumers are now realizing they have given away too much about themselves: So many companies now demand your mother's maiden name for security purposes that many banks recommend you *invent* a new, secret maiden name for her to ensure your bank account is secure.

Some consumers have already been horribly exposed: those who used Usenet in the nineties to post comments about their personal medical issues thought they were doing so privately, and used their real names. Today all those personal medical histories are just *one click away* on search engines.

How secure is your WiFi connection?

Not the main issue for marketing

For marketing though, we suspect that there is another, even more important privacy issue.

The issue of *price-sensitive information.*

THE CONSUMER'S COMMUNICATIONS BILL OF RIGHTS

1. Tell me clearly who you are, and why you are contacting me.
2. Tell me clearly what you are, or are not, going to do with the information I give you.
3. Don't pretend that you know me personally. You don't know me; you know some things about me.
4 Don't assume that we have a relationship.
5. Don't assume that I want to have a relationship with you.
6. Make it easy for me to say "yes" and "no."
7. When I say "no," accept that I mean not this, not now.
8. Help me budget not only my money, but also my time.
9. My time is valuable, don't waste it.
10. Make my shopping experience easier.
11. Don't communicate with me just because you can.
12. If you do that, maybe we will then have the basis for a relationship.

Lester Wunderman

Price-sensitive information

If you're a car salesman, getting a phone number or an address from the guy browsing in your showroom can be good, because you can then follow up a week later and send him brochures.

But the one bit of information that would really help you, and the one bit of information he will never tell you, is that he totaled his car yesterday, *and needs to drive off with another one before the beginning of the week.*

Know this, and your price negotiation will change out of all recognition.

Easy to detect

Online, it is increasingly easy to pick up this type of information:

> If you are a low cost airline, most of your customers come via the web.
>
> When they do, you offer then a price per seat on your flight depending on how full it is and how many days left you have to sell the seats.
>
> But what happens if they check your price, then go away and come back a day later?
>
> You can surmise that they will have checked out a few alternatives, and that they are coming back to you having decided to fly, and knowing that your price is lowest.
>
> So should you offer them the same price you offered them yesterday? Or should you offer them a slightly higher price, because *you know that they want to buy, and have no cheaper alternative?*

Many people type their passwords, bank account numbers and other details into little sticky note programs on computers.

Little do they know that some shareware sticky note programs share that information with other computers.

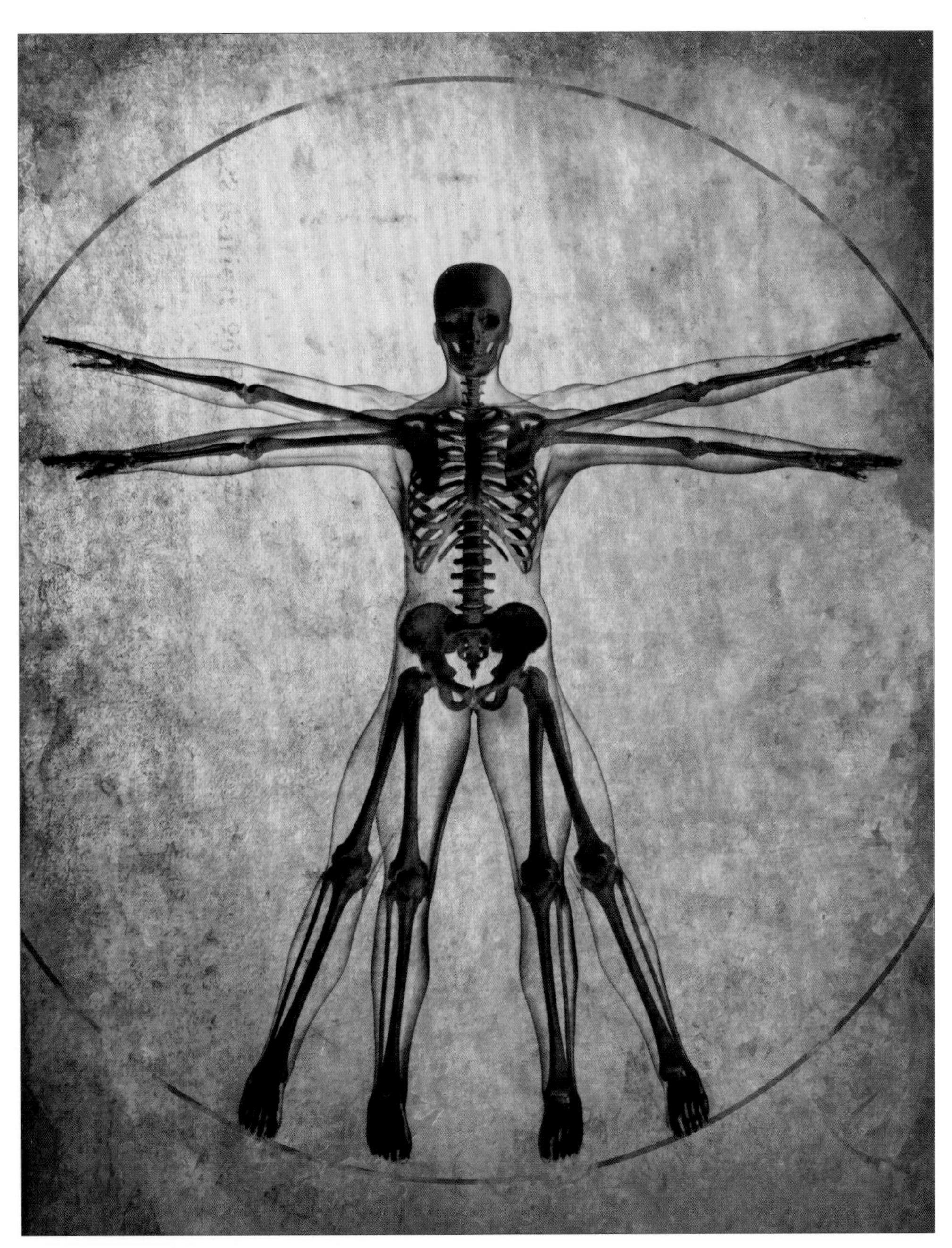

One day soon, some enterprising scientist will connect people's DNA with their search histories and clickstreams.

And the concept of free will, which has sustained mankind and its philosophers since the Renaissance, will no longer be so certain.

An airline that follows the second policy will make a lot more money than the one that sticks to its headline price.

Is this ethical? Low cost airlines already adjust their seat prices continually by a procedure known as 'load management' to ensure they maximize the profit made on each flight. All they are doing here is adjusting pricing depending on how much their customer needs to fly.

Everyone will face these ethical issues soon:

- You know from your pay-per-click analysis that certain keywords produce prospects who are much more interested in buying your wares than others. So should you charge the more interested people a *higher price?*
- Similarly, what if they come to your website from a competitive website? Do you offer them a *lower price* because you know they're looking around rather than just buying?

Expect this issue to grow and grow as software gets smarter.

'We're arresting you because we know that 50% of the people with your search history have gone on to commit serious crimes.'

Thought crime is only a few years away.

13. HOW DIGITAL MEDIA NEED TO EVOLVE

Search connects buyers and sellers at the moment the buyer expresses their need.

As such, it one of the most interesting marketing media ever invented.

Search is getting more intelligent or 'semantic', as engines keep developing, learning to understand contexts rather than just words.

It's also getting more visual, as engines work out ways of cataloging video.

But is it going in the right direction for commercial use?

Search needs to change

Current search engines are weak because:

1. They don't know *where* you are. The better ones know what country you are in, and that helps. But when you are looking for a motel for tonight, the results would be a lot more relevant if they knew

The best lover knows more about you than you do yourself.
If only the same were true of search engines.

that you were on Interstate 80 fifteen miles west of Lake Tahoe.

2. They don't know *who* you are. Even sophisticated online bookstores get it wrong. You buy a big pile of books on Dilbert, because you like Dilbert, and then you buy a Hannah Montana DVD set for your niece who likes Hannah Montana. So after that, the bookstore keeps recommending you stuff for the weird sort of person who likes both Dilbert and Hannah Montana.
3. They don't know *what drives you.* Most search engines know nothing about you apart from the search term you've entered. It would help that when you type in 'cash', the search engine knew whether you were looking for an ATM or for country music.
4. They don't know *more about you than you do yourself.* The best lover buys you a birthday present you didn't expect because that lover knows more about you than you do. Search engines would be really useful if they could do the same with search results, unmasking *latent desires.*
5. They expect you to search by *typing in words.* Why can't you just point and click like normal? If you see a sofa you like in a virtual world, you should be able to click on it and find one to buy.

Indeed, the next development in search engines may well be the more 'lean back' search engine. People already tend to type 'ebay' into search engines because they can't be bothered typing 'www.ebay.com'

Not all valuable innovation in mobile phones has been hi-tech. Part of the huge success of 2005's Motorola V3 RAZR was its ability to keep working and keep looking good after spending a year in a pocket full of keys and coins.

Satnav devices, linked to online services like MSN Direct, could make you geographically-relevant offers.

They should be a powerful new marketing medium.

The West needs a system that allows mobile phones to photograph and read barcodes, like the one that has become universal in Japan.

PLEASE SPEAK SLOWLY. I WAS BORN IN THE 1970s.

People born in the 1970s don't understand technology as fast as young people.

Simpler e-media could help them.

into their web browser. Further waves of convenience and laziness are sure to come.

As this happens, search engines will become less about active, committed search.

The value of individual clicks will go down.

But the end result will be that search will become a more powerful marketing tool.

Other developments needed

A hundred new media appear every year. Few offer useful marketing opportunities.

Here are a few new media that would help:

1. In the US and Europe, *a connection between paper and the mobile phone is needed.* In Japan, cameraphones that photograph and interpret barcodes on paper objects are commonplace, and a massively used consumer-friendly direct response system. Mobile service providers: if you want m-commerce to take off, ask the handset makers to work on this feature.
2. *Media that know where you are.* Cellphones tried to do location-based services in the 90s by tracking the cellphone tower the user was closest to, but it wasn't precise enough. Today, web browsers try to do the same thing by tracking the computer's IP address, but this isn't very accurate either. They can tell if you're in Seattle, but New York and New Jersey are just a blur. Soon we shall have the technology though - with 2-metre accuracy on GPS

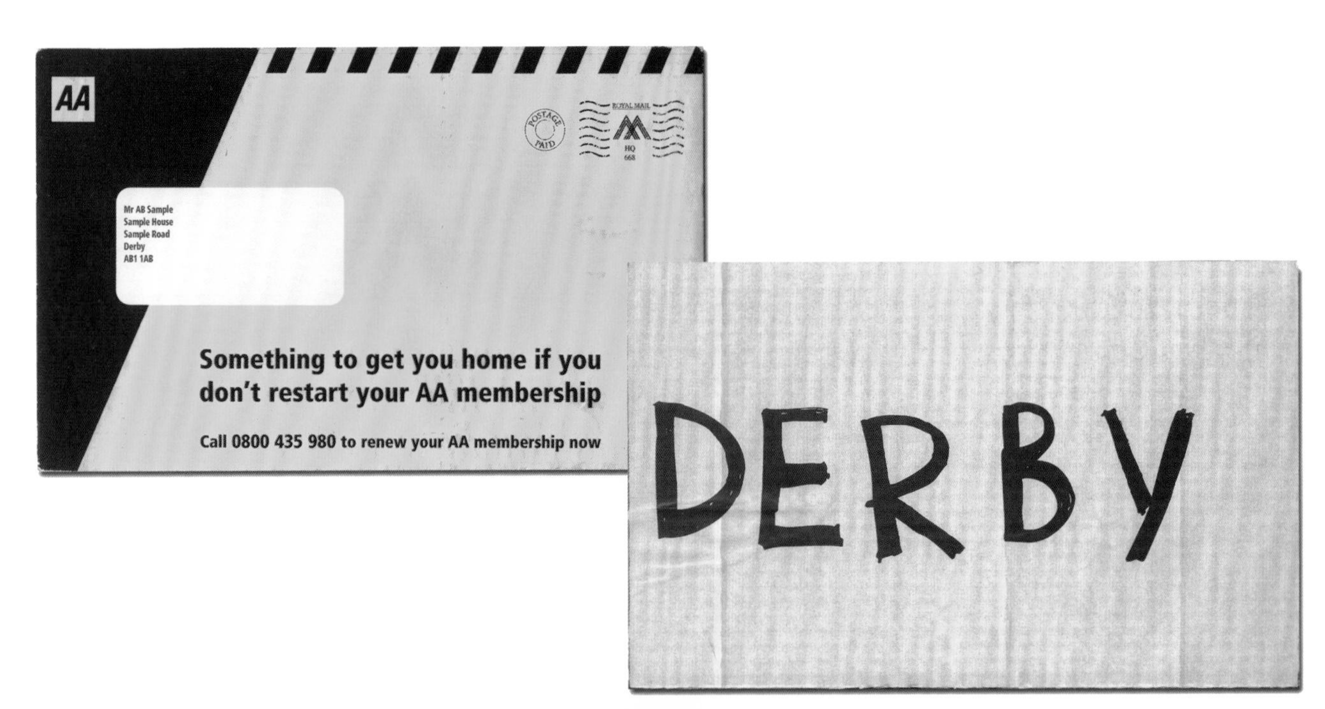

Not all digital media come on screens: When Britain's Automobile Association wanted a smart way of reminding members to renew their breakdown insurance, Wunderman London sent them digitally printed cardboard signs to help those who didn't renew to hitch a lift home.

chips a dollar each. The way some satnavs download MSN Direct data points the way.

3. Smart ad serving to set top boxes. We understand Google and News International are working on it.
4. Permission marketing media with an easy off button. We've found that many consumers like the idea of permission marketing - if they are thinking of going on vacation, the idea of divulging their needs and a budget and asking holiday companies to pitch at them is attractive. But too many permission marketers conceal their 'off' button, or ask you to remember a website password before you can stop the torrent of emails.
5. Smart spam filters - that allow stuff you want through, rather than block all commercial messaging. People who like Star Wars don't mind receiving mailings from purveyors of life-size imperial stormtrooper dolls.
6. No brainer e-media for people born in the 1970s. People born before 1980 don't use e-media nearly as fluidly as young people.
7. Standards in mobile phones. The 2G GSM standard let 2G phones rocket across Asia and Europe, leaving the US behind. But a lack of standards in smart 3G phones is hampering the development of e-media applications.

Virgin Atlantic send their most frequent flyers personalized, digitally printed cards on their birthday.

14. HOW TO PREDICT THE FUTURE

In 1999/2000 a trillion dollars of venture capital, savings and pensions evaporated in the dotcom bust.

The problem was, in the words of Alan Greenspan, 'irrational exuberance', a tendency by investors to believe the hype of companies that had no assets, no products, no customers and no sensible business plan.

In 1999, even smart people invested in pointless dotcoms. They operated on the 'greater fool' theory, that they could create a company, bring it to IPO, and get out before the house of cards collapsed.

And everyone knew of a greater fool. Wall Street thought it was retail investors. American retail investors thought they could sell their bubble stocks on to Europeans.

In the end, everyone got burned, and technology, media and telecoms went into a five-year depression.

The ability to keep one's head in the middle of such exuberance is not easy.

Consumers suffer from 'shiny object syndrome', a temporary attraction to new tech ideas, products and services that contain no benefit to them.

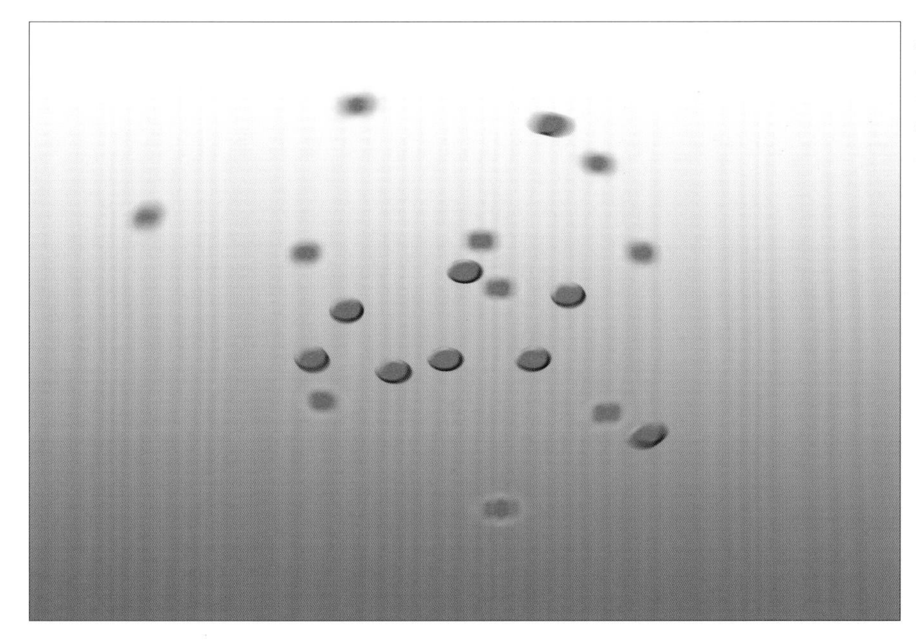

As Steve Jobs argued at the 2005 Stanford Commencement Ceremony, the dots that form your destiny only join up when you look back at them.

If investors in 1820s Britain had predicted the railways, they might not have blown their fortunes building canals.

Even consumers get swept up in new technology, so it's difficult to get a fix on what their real needs are:

- During the dotcom boom, focus groups of people whose daily routine consisted of get up, flip burgers for eight hours, watch TV, go back to sleep were convinced that they all needed a PDA to organize their life.
- Others were convinced that they would be doing all their shopping via the web. By 2001, they said in focus groups, Main Street would be history.

So how do you tell?

So how do you judge whether a new technology, gadget or web idea is going to be a long term winner?

Rapid initial sales are no guide to *long term* success.

Nor are focus groups. Or product tests.

Perhaps we need to go back to the basics of human progress.

Adam Smith, the father of economics, noted that human progress always involved *the division of labor:*

- When man divided the chores of agriculture and hunting, mankind progressed.
- When those in agriculture split again into farmers, millers and bakers, mankind progressed further.
- And as they specialized, their skills in the thing they focused on rose, and their skills in the thing they no longer did *disappeared.*

It was that disappearance that made progress permanent - the baker could not relapse to being a

In Vienna, you now pay for parking by texting your car registration number to a central computer.

Is cash dying?
In some cities, twentysomething women no longer carry it.

hunter gatherer because *he had never learned how to hunt.*

In 1999, some investment analysts were predicting the end of shopping on Main Street by 2005.

Today

Today, the division of labor happens less between people, and more between people and machines.

And as technology moves forward, the sign of permanent adoption is when someone no longer does something.

- Mobile phones are a permanent fixture of our lives because people can no longer operate their business and personal lives without them.
- iPods are a permanent fixture of the music scene because so many people have eBayed their CD collections.
- The jury is still out on social networking, because it hasn't replaced anything yet. (apart, of course, from working.)

So

So, if you are looking for permanent digital change, look for what people *aren't doing,* as much as what they are.

HANDLE TRIPLE PLAY WITH CARE

One of the biggest digital marketing issues of 2007 has been how to handle the bundling of landline and mobile telecoms with broadband and digital TV in packages known as 'triple play' and 'quadruple play'.

Here are our thoughts on the matter:

1. The multiple play offer is only as strong as its weakest component. Offer free broadband with a mobile plan and then fail to deliver it properly, and your customers won't like their new triple-play package one bit.
2. No one believes broadband speed promises any more, ever since they worked out that 'up to 8Mb' actually means 2.7Mb maximum. Work on rebuilding trust with your customers.
3. Wunderman's BrandAsset Valuator research shows that the strongest brands in the triple play universe are not broadband providers, or TV channels, or mobile service providers. They are the strong TV content brands like *Lost, Grey's Anatomy* or *The Simpsons.* Content is king - but only if you've got good content.
4. Terrestrial TV channels will be pushing you to offer terrestrial TV down your mobiles, to shore up their declining ratings. Don't assume this is as valuable as they think it is.
5. Your digital TV had better be easy to use. Consumers don't understand most of their existing remotes.
6. Don't stomp all over your customers if they try to leave. Churn is bad. But a reputation for obstructiveness builds fast online, and never goes away.
7. Many people under 30 don't have a landline, and will never have a landline. Build this thinking into your offers, rather than trying to force a landline down their throats to appease your copper-wire era CEO.
8. Your triple play offer is based on the bundle principle that 1+1+1 equals more than three. Not necessarily with your brand. Wunderman research in Hungary indicates that triple play brands can be a lot weaker that the brands they come from.
9. Don't assume that your sexy youth-oriented mobile service provider brand is as cool as it was in the 90s. Our BrandAsset Valuator image research suggests that AT&T was right to dump Cingular and select AT&T as its wireless brand name.
10. Giving people a DVR completely stops churn at satellite TV companies. If stopping churn is the objective of your triple play bundle, make this your priority instead.
11. Work out a better usage policy than just 'fair use'. For some service providers, 'fair use' means around 4GB of downloads a month. Anyone who buys a season of a TV series for their iPod from the US iTunes store will need 12GB in 24 hours.
12. And anyone who subscribes to HDTV downloads will need 12GB over and over. Keeping your customers over the next few years will mean constantly increasing the bandwidth you offer.

15. DEVELOP A CLOSER RELATIONSHIP WITH THE TRUTH

Nowadays, sales assistants in electrical stores like people who don't understand computers.

They go into the store, listen to the sales assistant and come out with what that assistant recommends them.

Not so the wired

The wired though are different, and sales assistants don't like them.

The wired first visit search engines, clicking on pay-per-clicks and price-comparison sites.

They then come into the store knowing the entire feature set of every item in the market, what they think of those features, what features they need, and exactly what they want to pay.

For the wired, digital media have *completely changed shopping.*

Also in services

Bad hotels don't like wired people either.

Five years ago, all they had to do was get a photographer to take some nice pictures of the hotel, write some glowing sales copy, get some brochures printed and suck up to their local tourism minister to get it a four star rating.

20th Century marketing was full of overclaim. In the 21st Century, the consumer can easily check whether what you say is true.

Today, none of this works:

- Many of the wired book their trips via Expedia or Travelocity. The hotel says it's quiet and has four stars. Its past visitors though say that there were teens running through the corridors all night and a guy selling crystal meth by the front door.
- Even people who book travel traditionally through shops have changed. They visit a travel agent and take down their suggestions. They then Google the suggested hotels, and check out user reviews on websites before confirming their booking.

In the past, the bad hotel could get people to stay once, but not twice.

Now they can't even get them to stay *once.*

In the digital age, what you deliver and what you don't is transparent to the consumer. So, if you don't want your marketing to sound like bullshit, it had better reflect the truth:

1. So tell the truth

Classical marketing training tells marketers to conceal or ignore defects in their product or service.

But faced with a consumer with a much better understanding of their wares and the marketplace, marketers who want to connect with them need to admit defects as well as sell benefits.

For many, this is not easy.

In the digital world, the guests checking into your hotel tonight are in touch with those who checked out last night.

2. Talk plain English

Classical marketers live in a world called 'marketingland' where consumers talk about and value the benefits they receive and respond in logical, controlled terms to the messages marketers fire at them.

In the new transparent world of digital, they need to adopt *the same language as their customers.*

3. Learn to cope with criticism

Chrysler thought SUVs were about performance, nature and comfort.

Until they encouraged consumers to create their own Chevy Tahoe commercials on their website.

And found that to consumers, SUVs were about *climate change* and *destroying the planet.*

4. And acquire a sense of humility

As blogosphere research by VML has discovered, when consumers discuss remodeling their kitchen, they aren't discussing the brand of paint they are going to use, they are discussing the *color.*

Most of the time, consumers don't discuss brand issues positively *or* negatively. Most don't discuss brand issues at all.

Marketers need to understand that as far as the consumer is concerned, *it's not necessarily about them.*

16. THE CONSUMER IS IN CONTROL – FOR NOW

Ten years ago, Ann decided to buy a sofa.

She vaguely remembered a furniture shop's TV jingle.

She also noticed that same furniture shop's price ad in the newspaper and thought that they might have some bargains for her.

So she drove to the furniture shop, picked a sofa in the right color, and bought it.

Ann based her decision mainly *on the furniture store's marketing.*

Today

Today, Ann's sofa is worn out.

She decides to buy a new one.

But this time the way she does it is very different:

- She looks at an online magazine, and starts thinking about colors and styles.
- She plays around with a feature on a home decoration website that allows her to pick sofa styles and try them in a *3-D rendering* of her living-room.
- She also looks at *user reviews,* and reads about how some furniture companies have good after-sales service and others don't. And how some furniture shops lie to you about delivery dates.
- She also picks up some *negotiation tips* from people who bought sofas from the same shop in the last month.
- She also looks at a *price comparison* website and works out where the cheapest places are for the sofa styles she likes.

This time, Ann makes a much more informed decision, based on a full 360 degree understanding of the sofa marketplace.

She still hears the furniture shop's jingle on TV, and once again she glances at its press ad covered in starbursts.

But this time round, the furniture shop's marketing plays *only a small part in her decision.*

Wired consumers are changing commerce all over the world.

So?

Pundits say that the consumer is in control today.

That's one way of putting it.

It's perhaps better to say that marketers are still using bows and arrows.

Whilst the consumer is now driving a tank.

Consumers are in the driving seat

The new supremacy of consumers is illustrated by the so-called 'user generated content' revolution.

In the digital era, marketers are still using bows and arrows.

Whilst the consumer is driving a tank.

- Consumers, armed with cameraphones, digital camcorders and laptop video editing are producing much more compelling and entertaining content than many advertising agencies and TV companies.
- Consumer generated content is having an amazing impact on some brands' sales. Sales of Mentos mints have gone through the roof since YouTube users discovered that they reacted with cola to create thirty-foot cola fountains.
- It can also be entertaining. The YouTube series about Darth Vader forced to be a supermarket night manager compares well in terms of plot and entertainment value with *Star Wars 1: The Phantom Menace.*

But the real question is: will this continue, or will media companies and marketers catch up and use digital media as effectively as the material some consumers are producing that the moment?

Analog user-generated content.

Marketers have a choice

Marketers can accept that the consumer is a much more powerful and much better connected player in the marketplace today.

And allow that consumer to control their prospects.

Or they can use their marketing money in much smarter ways.

Ensuring that the money is focused on the moment of truth.

Ensuring that the entire experience it delivers works.

Ensuring that no customers get screwed by unscrupulous sales people. Or a lazy product returns department. Or unhelpful delivery men.

In short, marketers can choose to raise their game or die.

And if they choose to raise it, they then need to keep raising it, as Moore's Law allows marketers and consumers to play increasingly sophisticated games with each other.

Some marketers may be terrified by this new circumstance.

But for others, it's going to be an exciting ride.

17. THE POWER OF NOW

When Sergio Zyman ran marketing at Coca-Cola, he said that his ambition was to put Coca-Cola within an arm's reach of anyone feeling thirsty.

The cost of making this happen was high – it meant distributing Cola-Cola to many more outlets.

But Coke was a marketing-led company, and so they did it anyway.

And Coke's sales rocketed.

Why did it work?

Zyman's move worked because there is a huge additional demand for things we can have now than there is for things that we have to wait for:

- Impulse travel websites like Lastminute.com have grown the travel market because there is huge latent demand for holidays you can go on *tonight.*
- Consumers send ten emails and texts for every letter they used to mail in the eighties, because whilst letters took 24 hours to arrive, emails and texts arrive *instantly.*
- Similarly, FedEx grew the package delivery market with a promise to deliver not in days, but *absolutely, positively overnight.*

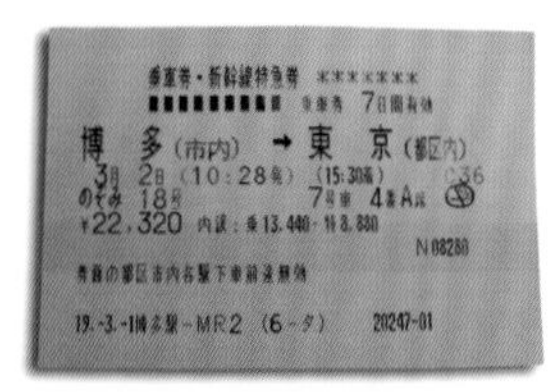

Rail and air passengers often pay a huge premium for tickets that let them travel immediately.

When you want a burger,
you want it now.

- Rich people may love waiting half an hour whilst a Michelin starred chef prepares their meal, but the mass of the population prefers a burger they can sink their teeth into *within minutes* of spotting a storefront.

The scale of the additional demand created by instant satisfaction can be seen when a burger joint gets crowded. Watch people desert the back of the queue as the wait makes them realize they *didn't really want a burger anyway.*

The *huge price premium* consumers will pay for instant satisfaction can be seen in hotels. In their rooms, guests pay ten dollars each for Snickers, Pringles or Coke from minibars. Outside the hotel, the same items sell for *a dollar each.*

Mobile service providers have charged so much for data downloads in recent years, that an average book would cost a fortune to download.

This has limited the prospects of 3G data services severely.

Good for digital products

As Coca-Cola found, it takes a lot of effort to deliver physical products and services instantly.

But the same is not true of digital ones. Bit-based products like ringtones, movies and music can be delivered easily, instantly, all over the world.

Satisfying demand instantly with digital products is therefore likely to have *a big future.*

The future of Hollywood

The latent demand concealed within instant satisfaction could be the savior of Hollywood and the music industry as they quake before their inevitable Napsterization.

Today though, Hollywood and the record industry spend more time worrying about protecting their product from piracy than they do developing additional revenues from instantly delivering films, music ringtones and other digital products.

They need to shift their focus:

- Whilst the record industry struggles to maintain CD sales, bands themselves are making more and more money out of concert tours. Why don't record companies consider selling live downloadable recordings of those concerts, perhaps only to those present and only within 24 hours of the concert? Someone who pays $200 for a concert ticket will pay $30 to keep a recording of that concert.
- The fashion industry operated on two seasons a year, until Zara introduced much faster six week cycles. Similarly, digitization means that music could move into much faster sales cycles.
- The new music model of a band launching itself on MySpace, building a fanbase and then linking with iTunes to get direct sales, has few time barriers. In time, there is no reason why bands should not become famous *instantly.*
- And people would pay a lot of money for instant access to this week's big hit. People are like that with fashion. They will pay $200 for $20 sneakers, just because they are the ones of the moment.
- Why don't movies sell private views?

Why don't cinema tickets contain links to movie merchandise websites?

Bigger than the long tail

Instant delivery may result in sales larger than the so-called 'Long Tail' of consumer demand, which has led to growing sales of niche items like Afro-Cuban jazz on Amazon and of Star Trek memorabilia on eBay.

It'll also be more important for big companies, because they do not like launching low-volume niche products.

But will they get it?

It is extraordinarily difficult for big companies to recognize that there is real value in new, untested bit-based products:

- In 1980, IBM let a tiny new company called Microsoft retain all rights to the MS-DOS operating system they had created for the new IBM PC - because the value as they saw it lay in the hardware, not 'in floppy disks'.
- Similarly, mobile phone makers and network service providers focused on covers, cases and other physical phone accessories in the 1990s, and left ringtones on the table. Today, ringtone companies like Jamba have marketing budgets that exceed those of many telecoms companies.

For marketers in many industries, missing an opportunity to deliver instant digital satisfaction is likely to be the *biggest mistake of their career.*

Why doesn't the music industry ensure consumers have the right to re-download tracks they have bought whenever they need to?

The music industry says they can back up the tracks themselves. But as the computer industry knows, no one backs up.

18. BORING ISN'T BORING AT THE MOMENT OF TRUTH

When the web first became popular in 1997, life insurance companies became excited.

They could appeal to consumers through new, interactive, engaging media.

So they developed and launched websites.

They then looked at their visitor counts and wept.

Consumers didn't want to interact with insurance companies via the web any more than they did one hundred years previously when their salesmen forced an interactive foot through the consumer's front door.

Today

Today though, search is having a massive influence on

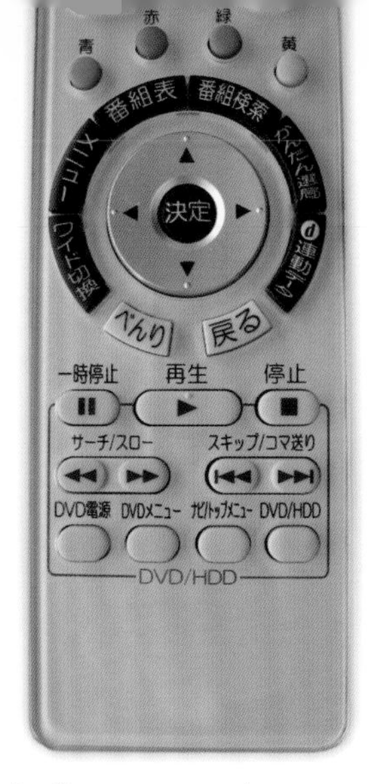

As the consumer becomes more and more adept at eliminating bad advertising and other stuff that bores them, the classical advertising of financial services companies will suffer disproportionately.

insurance companies, banks, lawyers, and other service categories.

Because at the moment of truth, *no product or service is boring.*

Most people spend their lives avoiding thinking about their own death, apart from the time when it suddenly hits them that they have dependents, who will need looking after if they die.

At this point, life insurance suddenly becomes the most interesting product in the world.

And consumers are willing to read *pages* about it.

This was never possible to do efficiently before.

Insurance companies had to mail out reams of prestigious brochures, and do thousands of expensive sales calls to find one prospect ready to think about life insurance or a pension.

Now, through search, they can find a steady source of those people, at the precise moment when they are interested in protecting themselves, their families or their future.

This is leading insurance companies to massive new efficiencies.

The efficiencies are there too for other services like lawyers. The most expensive word to buy on search engines is *mesothelioma* – the industrial disease people pick up from asbestos. Industrial injury lawyers pay as much as $30 a click to attract those diagnosed with the disease to their websites.

But with those $30 clicks, they can forget about spending thousands on advertising.

The clicks are the only marketing expense they need.

But

The only problem is, most of the websites that financial services firms then lead customers to are *incomprehensible:*

- Life insurance companies should think why the most successful tactic they have is to offer potential customers a free carriage clock to sign up. It's not because customers love carriage clocks. It's because the carriage clock is the *only part of the offer they understand.*
- Research shows that consumers don't really understand the calculations and projections that are the staple fare of life insurance websites. An onsite pension calculator is no bad thing. But if people don't understand what the results of the calculation mean, the website has failed.

In the digital age, it is time that brands in boring categories completely re-thought their marketing strategy.

Life insurance customers like the carriage clock because it's the only part of the offer they understand.

19. LOCALIZATION ISN'T JUST TRANSLATION

US-written software packages are usually launched in English, and then localized into other languages and cultures only once they are very successful.

This means that many people whose native tongue is not English end up using English-language software.

This has had an appalling influence on many languages.

When Germans pass on an email, they use the verb 'forwarden'.

Similarly, the Académie Française has just created a new French word for email. They couldn't stop people people saying 'une email' instead of 'un courrier électronique', so the new word is 'un mél'.

Today though, most of the software people use is available in forty or more languages, so these issues are over.

But there are still some glaring localization problems out there:

Despite the rise of globalization, eating habits remain local. In parts of Eastern Europe, pigs' ears remain a tasty appetizer.

In Indochina, rat meat remains a staple dish. Sauteed with a little lemongrass and oil, it tastes like light, fluffy chicken.

- Japanese tourists moan that whilst the rest of the world is full of web cafés, few have the Japanese language keyboards they need.
- In Ukraine, most people use SMS text to keep in touch with their friends. But most phones won't let them write in anything other than Latin letters. So they have to *transliterate* everything before they send it.
- Most US e-tailers continue to price goods exclusive of sales tax in their global stores, because that's they way they do it in America. European tourists visiting America though struggle with the fact that a $10 note won't buy a $10 item. Sales tax is always included in the sales total in Europe, and in most places outside the US. *When in Rome, do as the Romans.*
- In India, dating sites need to adapt to allow parental involvement in the dating process. In India, marriages arranged by parents are still common, even amongst the urban technocratic elite.
- Social networking sites assume that everyone lives in Western-style countries with liberal parents. Not so in the Arab world. Social networking sites must adapt to reflect much more conservative families in these countries.

Ukrainians and Russians use the Cyrillic alphabet. But when they text, many phones force them to use Latin characters.

The Wunderman Network has developed careful processes to ensure that digital marketing is localized fully. The basics are as follows:

1. Translation is only the beginning. The web presence

should feel like it was created *in the country for the country.*

2. People who have lived in a country know it much better than people who just speak the language. *Don't just rely on expats.*
3. Research everything amongst the end users. *And then research it again.*

Today, digital media are allowing companies to sell everywhere on Earth - *if only their marketing can keep up.*

Few web cafes outside Japan have the keyboards Japanese tourists need in order to write home.

20. JUST BECAUSE IT'S DIGITAL DOESN'T MEAN IT'S BETTER

You're a business executive in a foreign country.

You're in a taxi heading for the airport.

The traffic's backing up.

You know you're going to miss your flight.

Should you continue to the airport in the hope that there's another flight today?

Or give up and head back to your hotel?

NASA spent millions developing pens that pumped ink to the tip, so they still worked in zero gravity.

The Russians just used a pencil.

You choose

In the 21st century, you have three ways of deciding:

- You can fire up your laptop, find an unsecured wifi hotspot next to the freeway and access your airline's timetables via the web.
- You can hope that your mobile phone contract

allows you to access 2.5G data services abroad, and use it to surf to the airline's wap portal.

- Or you can phone the airline's voicemail system from your mobile, and between bursts of static, speak the names of departure airport, arrival airport and time of departure to the computer voice system, and hope it gives you flight details back.

Of course, none of these state-of-the-art digital methods usually work.

None of the peripherals you bought for your old computer work with your new one.

So why should the digital-rights-managed music?

Compare that with ten years ago

Compare that with ten years ago, when business travelers just reached into their bag for one of the timetables airlines gave away at every check-in desk.

The printed timetables worked fine.

But they no longer exist - because the airlines have gone digital.

Digitization is making airline service go *backwards.*

It's the same with music

Similarly, the music industry has developed digital-rights-managed music for the digital era that is *less portable and less secure* than the CD that you bought ten years ago.

And with travel agents

And business travel agents today supply all itineraries via weblinks. 'You can download them on to your PDA' they say. But the links don't work with most PDAs. The schedule is only good if you are in front of an internet enabled PC with a printer attached.

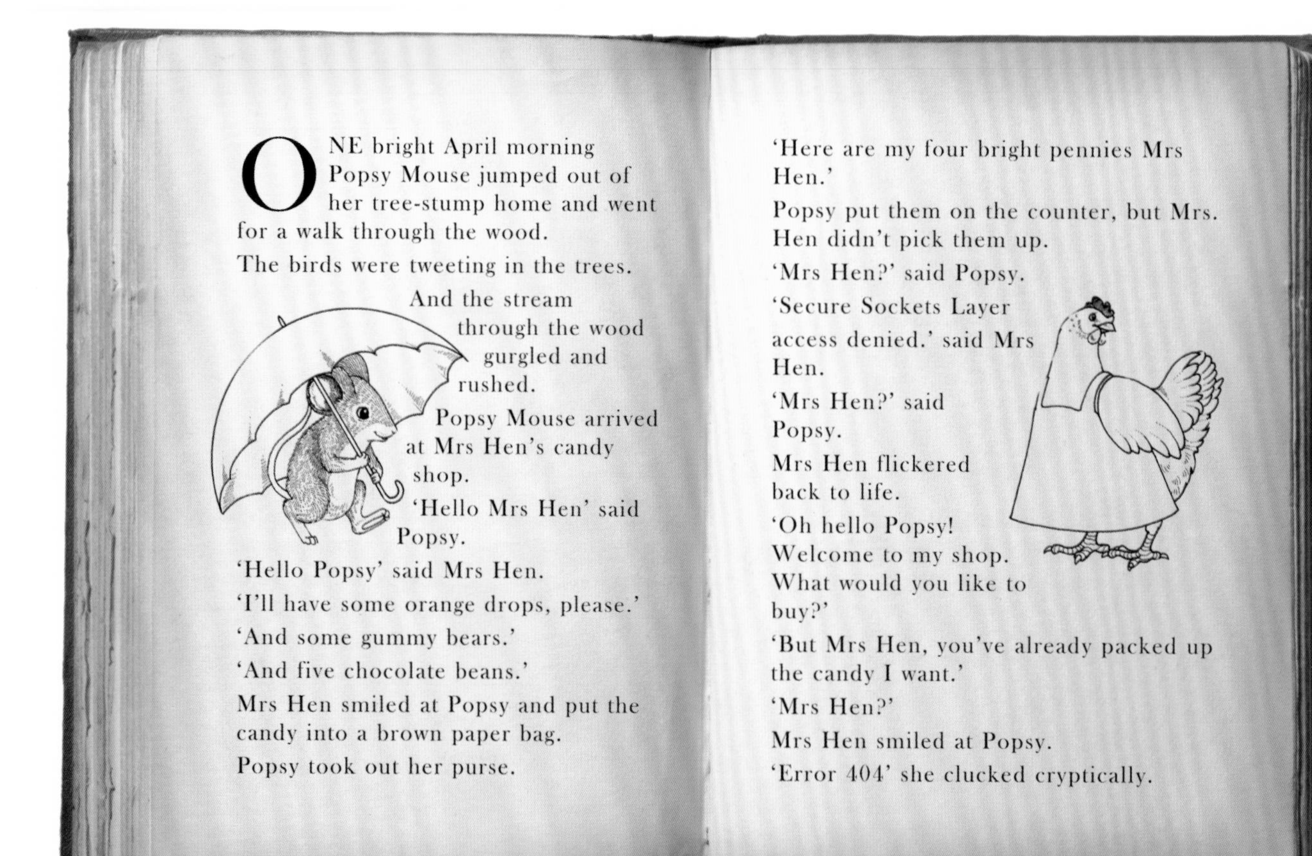

ONE bright April morning Popsy Mouse jumped out of her tree-stump home and went for a walk through the wood.

The birds were tweeting in the trees.

And the stream through the wood gurgled and rushed.

Popsy Mouse arrived at Mrs Hen's candy shop.

'Hello Mrs Hen' said Popsy.

'Hello Popsy' said Mrs Hen.

'I'll have some orange drops, please.'

'And some gummy bears.'

'And five chocolate beans.'

Mrs Hen smiled at Popsy and put the candy into a brown paper bag.

Popsy took out her purse.

'Here are my four bright pennies Mrs Hen.'

Popsy put them on the counter, but Mrs. Hen didn't pick them up.

'Mrs Hen?' said Popsy.

'Secure Sockets Layer access denied.' said Mrs Hen.

'Mrs Hen?' said Popsy.

Mrs Hen flickered back to life.

'Oh hello Popsy! Welcome to my shop. What would you like to buy?'

'But Mrs Hen, you've already packed up the candy I want.'

'Mrs Hen?'

Mrs Hen smiled at Popsy.

'Error 404' she clucked cryptically.

Thankfully, traditional commerce isn't like much of today's digital commerce.

And with corporations

Most corporations serve their customers much worse now that they have replaced their switchboard operators with voicemail jails.

So

Companies thinking of developing new digital customer handling systems had better be careful that digitization means their quality of service goes *up*, not *down:*

- If you offer a financial service, and your customers visit your site only once a year to renew, think carefully about how you let them in. No consumer remembers a password for a year.
- If you are an airline, make sure a link to your timetables is prominent on your homepage.

  If your website is run by your e-commerce team, they may be tempted to force people looking for plane times through the e-booking engine, in the hope that they might buy a ticket online instead.
- Consider using CRM software to manage your customers. As the cost of human contact rises and rises, smart CRM software is *the future of service.*

Why is it that you only get to talk to a helpful, live human being on most customer care voicemail systems when you select the 'open a new account' option?

21. ALL WARFARE IS BASED ON DECEPTION

Marketing directors are used to standing up and telling the world about their marketing strategies.

In the TV era, this was fine.

Their creative strategies were all up there on TV for the world to see.

Their media strategies didn't vary more than 10% from brand to brand.

But that's not the way other strategists work.

In the military, secrecy, subterfuge and deception are what strategy is all about.

In guerrilla warfare

In January 1968, North Vietnamese forces surrounded the U.S. military base at Khe Sanh.

The U.S. made huge efforts to reinforce the base, to ensure it could not be taken.

But the attack never came.

The siege was purely a diversion for the Tet Offensive,

If you come up with a powerful new way of using digital media, don't tell the world about it.

the Viet Cong's assault on 200 towns and cities in South Vietnam which destroyed the U.S. public's belief that victory in Vietnam was possible.

In world wars

In 1944, the Nazis placed huge troop concentrations around Calais in France, to oppose General Patton's huge U.S. first tank army waiting to cross the English Channel.

But Patton's tanks were inflatable copies.

The real invasion fleet landed in Normandy.

In search

Similarly today, the great successes of the digital age have often happened before the world in general realized anything was happening.

Google built its hugely dominant position in paid search whilst it was a private company and didn't have to tell the world what it was doing.

A smart general doesn't tell his enemy what he's about to do.

Today, most of the marketing world *still* doesn't understand what they did and how they did it.

Similarly, MySpace's success in social networking happened before it appeared on the marketing radar.

So

So we could tell you more about the big successes we

are achieving in the digital space for Wunderman Network clients.

We could then impress you with our Adaptive Marketing Engine database marketing programs.

Our behavioral targeting techniques.

And our interactive Customer Relationship Management tools.

As we say, we could tell you all of this.

But then we'd have to kill you.

ABOUT THE WUNDERMAN NETWORK

Wunderman is the most diverse digital relationship marketing network in the world.

We help the most powerful brands reach customers wherever they are to inspire action, lifelong relationships and deliver measurable results.

In a world that doesn't stand still, best-in-class talent thrive on opportunities from new marketing technologies and have the speed and flexibility that help ensure rapid decision-making supports intelligent and successful market building for our clients.

World class analytics teams constantly measure and optimize communications across all media.

Daily, and even hourly updates enable quick reactions to unexpected market forces.

We have the data, processing, analytics, campaign management and reporting resources to continuously evaluate and refine campaign elements and enable our clients to be as dynamic and competitive as the environment in which they operate.

If you would like to learn more about Wunderman, please visit www.wunderman.com.

VML

blast radius

studiocom

SHAW WUNDERMAN